AF869027

GOVERNMENT, JUSTICE, AND CONTEMPT

GILLES LANE

UNIVERSITY PRESS OF AMERICA

Lanham • New York • London

Copyright © 1993 by
University Press of America®, Inc.
4720 Boston Way
Lanham, Maryland 20706

3 Henrietta Street
London WC2E 8LU England

All rights reserved
Printed in the United States of America
British Cataloging in Publication Information Available

Library of Congress Cataloging-in-Publication Data

Lane, Gilles.
[Pouvoir, justice et non-mépris. English]
Government, justice, and contempt / Gilles Lane.
p. cm.
Includes index.
1. Justice. 2. Political science—Philosophy. I. Title.
JC578.L3513 1993 320'.01'1—dc20 92–34527 CIP

ISBN 0–8191–8956–1 (cloth : alk. paper)
ISBN 0–8191–8957–X (pbk. : alk. paper)

The paper used in this publication meets the minimum requirements of American National Standard for Information Sciences—Permanence of Paper for Printed Library Materials, ANSI Z39.48–1984.

CONTENTS

PREFACE

Many people are inclined to think, on certain occasions, that if everyone in our society pursued his or her own projects without harming the others, or preventing them from realizing their own pursuits, then each one of us would be living the happiest life we could possibly live. As a matter of fact, leaving aside accidents and physical as well as psychological illness, it would seem that the greatest obstacle to a happy life, for everyone, is precisely this harmful behavior of some of the others.

The same people are also convinced, of course, that life would be happy for an even greater number of people if, apart from not harming any others, everyone were concerned about *helping* those who have to suffer a rather painful life, at least when that could be done without one's own chances for a happy life being too seriously threatened.

Here, then, is a belief that is widespread, if not always very conscious. It is actually confirmed, to a certain extent, by the fact that everyone feels, on various occasions, a *moral obligation* to avoid harming others, and even to assist them in times of need. Some have interpreted this moral feeling as pointing to yet another fact: all human beings would not only have the desire, but also the *right* to live as happy a life as possible, that is, a life whose happiness would be limited only by the normal capacities of each and every one of us. (One might even think that without the existence of such a right, it would sometimes be difficult to understand how we could feel *really* obliged to refrain from causing any harm at all — even a small one — to other people.)

Since it so happens, however, that many of us often do cause harms to others — whether aware of it or not —, most people therefore believe it would be a great loss, a real calamity, if there didn't exist a "government", or some form of power capable of forcing everyone, when necessary, to refrain from violating the apparently universal and basic human right to a decently happy life. It isn't only the barely educated people, or the supposedly naive, who share this more or less spontaneous belief, but also a good number of the scientists and other specialists who are nowadays searching for solutions to the problems of life in our societies. At first sight, then, it would seem perfectly natural, or not in the least surprising, that such beliefs did exist.

What could very well be surprising, however, is the fact that no one seems to experience any real doubts concerning the *possibility* of living in agreement with those beliefs. (That fact was at the origin of the present book.) One may indeed wonder how anyone lucid could continue to believe, after due reflection, that people *could* realize any particular project — whichever it may be! — *without* causing any harm to others, sooner or later. In other words, how could one believe it possible for anyone to lead a really happy life *without* others having to live a more difficult or painful one, as a consequence? With a bit of imagination, wouldn't anyone see that it is in fact impossible that the *concrete* developments of each person's projects for a happy life *never* interfered with those of the other persons, sometimes for the good fortune of some, of course, but often, also, for the *misfortune* of quite a few others?

What this book will try to offer is a possible answer to the following questions. Can a government itself (no matter which) avoid committing any act of *injustice*, while using force to keep certain citizens from causing damages to others? Is it even possible for a government, or any individual, to *know* if those who have caused damages to others have thereby committed real acts of *injustice*? On the other hand, do we know what a "really serious" harm or damage would be? Or what a "really" happy life would be, for each person? And if we did *not* know these things, how could we ever have a *sufficient* reason (or "the right") to do what would *perhaps* increase the chances of a happy life for certain persons, but perhaps also diminish — even seriously! — the same chances for other persons? How could a government have this "right" more than any other people, being itself just as much in the dark as anyone else about these matters? If ever we *could* have sufficient reasons to act in spite of this ignorance, *what is it* that would be giving their "sufficiency" to such reasons?

These questions are basically the same as the ones which many specialists are still trying to answer. But the more liberal thinkers never seem to succeed in reconciling the concrete rights and the liberty of each and every one of us, on the one hand, and a happy life *for all*, on the other hand. As for the social-minded thinkers, they believed to have found the actual solution to the problem of a happy life for the poor and the destitute, but could hardly reconcile this solution with everyone's *liberty*, especially with the liberty of the learned and the rich. Some of them would like to *impose* a common project on their own society as a whole, or on the entire world, and then simply "liquidate" the "subversive elements" until "all" human beings — those who remained! — might live a happy life without ever having to harm anyone... These difficulties are in fact insurmountable, but they result, as I shall contend, from a *misapprehension* of what would be more fundamentally at stake when moral rights and obligations (or justice itself) are concerned, or when the *real* obstacles to a happy life are brought into question.

The intuition that has guided this study is that it should not be necessary to know if a particular act is "in itself" just or unjust, or if its consequences will *in fact* be the least harmful, in order to know whether or not we would be doing something unjust in producing it. (Many seem to think it is, but at the cost of neglecting important parts of our daily experience.) Nor should it be necessary, in order to know this, that we waited for the common agreement of all the others, or of the greater number of experts on the matter. The reason is that it is often *at this very moment* that we would have to decide what to do, and therefore know well enough which choice would be just or unjust. To bring this intuition to its fullness would require, of course, that something *more immediately* knowable or attainable be found, something to which we could turn — or to which we perhaps do turn, but without always noticing that we do — in order to find out soon enough, and with the desired amount of certainty, how we would be able to act *without* doing anything unjust.

To reinforce this intuition while making use of it, I have adopted a very simple but rather demanding method. It aims at clarifying some of the so-called "substantive" elements of the beliefs already contained in our judgments concerning just or unjust behavior, and tries to bring out the fact that these elements logically imply the presence of still *other* beliefs. But even if the latter may serve to explain the former, the use of the selected method cannot, by itself, provide us with a fairly satisfying comprehension, if only because purely logical implications can never guarantee the existence of "substantive" or "worldly" objects. What would be needed, then, is that everyone verified for themselves[1] if *they* did, or did not have the implied experiences or beliefs (concerning justice, the happy life, or the possibility of these for *all* members of society). One could immediately notice, however, that if the outcome of this verification were to be a positive answer, then everyone would know right away what he or she may reasonably expect from life within a society, or from any political power, and above all, what no one could ever expect from either of them without any *illusion.*

* * *

The main results of this study may be summarized as follows. What is morally unjust is not simply to cause harms or damages to others, but to do so out of one's own *free* choice, and with a certain *contempt* towards the persons themselves. Even though all persons may therefore know if *they* do, or do not have the right to produce such and such an act (even against any "positive" law), they cannot but remain in the dark, however, as to whether *the others* do, or do not have the right to do what they do (no matter what!). — How indeed could we know if the others are in fact capable of a free choice, at this moment, and if their behavior is accompanied by a really *personal* contempt?

Not knowing this, of course, need not paralyze anyone, since it shouldn't be necessary, as some are apt to think, that we knew that the behavior of the others is

[1] The problems studied in this book happen to preoccupy many people who are not experts in the field of ethics and political philosophy, but are nevertheless quite capable of understanding — and even appreciating! — critical arguments and detailed discussions. Since I also wish *their* attention, and *their own* verification of the main points of this study, I have tried to use a language with which they would be quite familiar.

actually *unjust*, in order to have the right to force them to change it. It is enough that we truly believed we were able to make use of this force *without* any contempt towards the persons themselves.

The universal law (and therefore the "natural" law) of justice itself is not, then, a law of "non-harm", but rather, and more basically, a law of "non-contempt". It is in fact the manifestation of a belief which is not always clearly noticed but is nevertheless felt, since without its perception, no one could indeed consider as "sufficient", or even understandable, the reasons for which he or she believes that this particular act or behavior is, or is not unjust. In itself, this law is not purely relative or subjective, since each time it is felt, it imposes the *same* thing to everyone, that is, independently of each person's present desires, willful requirements, or factual impulses.

There is nothing arbitrary about the fact that our moral obligations of justice mainly concern the "non-contempt" of anyone's person. (More positively, justice requires "consideration", rather than mere non-contempt.) Since obligations of justice can only address themselves to persons who are capable of choosing *freely*, one may indeed note that, the conditions of possibility of free choices being what they are, these obligations cannot but somehow contain the basic obligation of avoiding all willful contempt towards any person. In other words, liberty itself could only arise when one is inevitably "facing" other persons, that is, the only kind of beings towards which it would be impossible, at times, *not* to adopt a *freely* chosen attitude either of consideration, *or else* of contempt.

In spite of many appearances and spontaneous fears, fulfilling all of one's various obligations of justice — and thereby maintaining one's practical concern for the others — cannot possibly condemn anyone to a really unhappy life, nor even to surrender his or her own chances for a happy future. On the contrary. It so happens, indeed, that the desire for an at least fundamentally happy life requires, for its satisfaction, that one led a *freely* chosen life, that is, a life which one's own person *itself* would have become interested in living. But precisely because the obligations to "consider" the others address themselves to our liberty — thereby calling it forth to existence, or increasing our awareness of it —, they also happen to promote a happy life for our persons themselves. And this, again, helps to understand *why* the presence of the other persons — which moral justice always obliges to "consider" — is needed not only for everyone to act freely, or quite personally, but also for everyone's person to *live* a happy life.

At this point, our study may allow us to foresee a possible answer to our first question: "What could be reasonably expected from a government, regarding policies that would benefit *all* the members of our society?". Certainly this much, at least: that the rulers strive to establish policies which would be apt to promote a mutual "consideration" between all citizens, that is, a life common to human beings living in a true "society". But if this mutual consideration is to be really nourishing for the persons as such, it would have to be actively shared through *concrete* facts, especially when the poor and the helpless are concerned... Those who govern — and who still *remain* fellow citizens! — would then have to find and, above all, to encourage definite ways of promoting a *mutual aid* between all citizens. If they did this, they would be doing, hopefully with an ever increasing number of citizens, what could best enable *all* the citizens (including themselves) to lead a more fundamentally happy life.

In any case, more people today are aware of the fact that persons, as such, need the "consideration" of the others, as they also need to offer them their own. (Throughout this book, the phrases "persons *as such*", or "persons *themselves*", will simply mean: whatever qualities, capacities, defects, or behavior the different human beings might otherwise have.) This particular awareness is undoubtedly the reason why striving to be a hard individualist, or to be autonomous (in the sense of being as much as possible independent of the others), is often perceived, nowadays, as a sign of unnatural contempt towards all persons. And one should certainly be allowed to count on such an awareness.

Precisely because of it, it seems that something *could* be done, after all, to improve everyone's life in what would then be a true *society*. In fact, all those who wish to participate in such a task — especially our political rulers and all our educators — could keep on doing what they are already doing for that purpose, but with a still more confident effort to promote — each according to his or her own capacities and style — a most universal concern for mutual "consideration" itself, and its natural expression, effective mutual aid.

This book was first written in French, and published in Montreal by V.L.B. (1989). I have rewritten it in English, while seizing the opportunity to omit certain parts, but also to add quite a few developments, and substantiate or elucidate many others. As a last comment, I would like to stress the fact that I have chosen to pursue the present study with a decidedly pluralistic intent. This simply means that I have limited my attention to topics, experiences, arguments, and beliefs that are *more commonly* human, and which could therefore be found acceptable, at least as subject matter for reflection, by readers of very *different* mentalities and convictions (such as those, let us say, of scientists and humanists, religious believers and non believers, liberals and socialists, and so on). Or that, at least, is my hope.

1. THE IMPOSSIBLE GOVERNMENT

At least in countries where no war is presently raging, most citizens see their government as a group of persons who have (or should have) a twofold task concerning the whole of society. In fact, it is normally expected from a government that it tried its best to increase the chances of a happier life for *all* the law-abiding citizens, including the less fortunate, and will therefore see to it that, in principle, not one of them will be seriously harmed *in the process itself*. But it is also expected from this same government — perhaps so that it may better accomplish the main part of its task — that it succeeded in reducing as much as possible the number of acts of *injustice* that everyone has to suffer, all too often, from some of the others, and that it did this without *itself* being unjust to any of the citizens.

If, according to most citizens, their government is capable in fact of realizing such a project, it would have to be on the following condition: that it should determine a certain number of things which all citizens would *have* to do (or to refrain from doing), having itself no other choice, thereafter, but to *force* them, if need be, to "obey" these indispensable laws. Moreover, most citizens are also convinced that their government does in fact possess a physical power which is superior to that of any other special group, and is thus capable of coercing all members of society into taking up any behavior it would like to see them adopt.

The difficulties of governing

In spite of what the majority of citizens believe, our governments are well aware of being quite unable to force everybody, at any time, to do or to refrain from doing any thing whatever. For example, to do things everyone would consider too painful to do; or to refrain from doing things everyone values enormously. Nor is it enough that government policies never demanded, from anyone, things that might be immediately painful to do. For a government knows it would indeed find it insurmountably difficult to have the citizens accept a policy which too many of them feared it would bring about, if only *later*, all sorts of harmful or unjust acts.

Governments are absolutely sure that to accomplish their social project — no matter which — they must be able to rely on a certain amount of cooperation coming from the citizens. They are also aware of having to set up laws and penalties which would be consistent not so much with their own conception of a happy life for everyone, or of what is just or unjust, but rather with the citizens' conceptions of these matters. And if not with the conceptions of the majority of them, then a least with those held by the minorities who really have the power to oppose their own government (either each one all by itself, or in conjunction with the other minorities). As a matter of fact, such groups could even force a government to yield its would-be "supreme" power, either to acquire it for themselves, or to have their friends do so.

(Of course, a government could carry out, to a certain extent, a project which actually went against the conceptions that most citizens have of a happy life, or of justice itself. But this could only work if, for example, that government managed to organize *early enough* a well compartmentalized secret police, a system of mutual denunciation, sudden "disappearances" and "deterring" torture, so as to establish a climate of fear and distrust that could most effectively discourage any organized reaction of self-defence... But this case, although notoriously important, won't be considered in the present study.)

It just isn't true, therefore, that governments are generally capable of doing what they would like, even if that consisted only in determining their own policies and forcing any citizen, or group of citizens, to comply with them. It still remains a fact, however, that most citizens think it *is* true, or at least behave as if they really thought it were. The reason is no doubt that they naturally interpret everything their government does, as trustworthy manifestations of the *supreme* power it pretends it has — so "supreme", in fact, that no other group of citizens could ever dare to defy it openly.

Despite the fact that governments absolutely need — and appreciate! — this particular belief of the citizens, it does cause them all kinds of difficulties. If, let us say, a government has not yet improved the fate of the more unfortunate, or if small groups of rich people are still keeping many other citizens from living a more decent life, or if acts of injustice are becoming ever more frequent and severe, then surely the reason must be — according to this belief of the citizens — that the government just *doesn't want* to change the situation. Isn't it true, after all, that the government has the greatest power, and therefore the means to coerce *anyone*? — How, then, could it *not* be considered as an accomplice to all these offensive acts or omissions?

Governments, of course, don't particularly like to answer that kind of questions by admitting that they would very much want to fulfill these normal expectations of the citizens, but are simply *incapable* of doing so. They know too well that the citizens just wouldn't believe them, or that perhaps they would, but only to vote the next time for more vigorous or more competent rulers...

If, because of this belief of the citizens, a government cannot succeed in getting itself acquitted in the minds of a good majority of them, or in persuading them to be patient, how, then, could this government obtain from them the *voluntary* cooperation it absolutely needs to be able to fulfill their expectations, and thereby exonerate itself? In other words, these difficulties would seem to indicate that the power of a government could only be *efficiently* "supreme" if a sufficient number of citizens happened to give it their consent. They also indicate that a government's *efficient* long-term projects could only be the ones that a vast majority of citizens approved, or adopted as their own, or had even forced that government to take up for itself.

One can well imagine how the political rulers could actually succeed in dissipating the impatience and mistrust of many citizens, and even in winning over their cooperation in all their projects for a better society, if only their attitude and their actual policies would show that they *really* wanted to work for society and *all* its members. But that would be overlooking a formidable obstacle, namely, the *secret* pressure that governments are subjected to, whenever they are deciding upon what is to become "their own" projects. This pressure — always intent on remaining secret — is exerted by organizations to which money, and the successful management of well-known establishments or corporations, have given an unbelievable amount of power. Of course, these establishments are of great service to society or to the government itself, at times, but they constantly threaten the political rulers of letting them down (or even of putting them out of a job!), should they ever refuse to favor *their* policies.

What these powerful groups require of a government, for an ever greater increase of their own profits, is that their threats remained absolutely secret, and that the government itself let the citizens believe that its policies were really *its own*, and always inspired by its own concern for *the whole* of society. But one can easily understand that such a pressure cannot but modify, to a large extent, the attitudes and especially the conduct that a government could otherwise have wished to adopt. And it therefore becomes impossible for the citizens to keep on believing and hoping that their government *still really wants* to establish the conditions of a happy life for *everyone*, as well as the conditions for the gradual disappearance of the worst kind of unjust behavior.

It is no wonder, then, that it should be more and more difficult for governments to obtain from the citizens a fair amount of trust, cooperation, and patience. Besides, the secret pressure groups can't have so very much to lose, as a matter of fact, from the downfall of any government, since all they have to do, each time, is to make sure that the next one will also "cooperate". They can even enjoy the advantages that usually come with each new start...

If every political ruler and every experienced politician knows very well that such are, in fact, the insurmountable difficulties that his or her own policies will encounter — whether or not these would be inspired by a true concern for *all* the citizens —, how, then, can such persons really *want* to acquire political power for themselves, or *persist* in wanting to preserve it? One of the answers to that question comes from the persons immediately concerned: they are constantly driven by their passionate desire to take on a *challenge*.

Intents and motives of political rulers

Many members of our governments actually have one aim, and only one, in wanting to occupy their position: to take on a personal challenge. Some will admit it without the slightest embarrassment. Every one of them constantly wants to try his or her luck, totally convinced of being a "winner" and particularly gifted, besides, to preside over the common destiny of their society. In any case, each one feels at least as able as many other people, and certainly more able than any adversary. (There lies the challenge!)

Just as determined and impassioned as the best athletes, these political rulers, and politicians, lose no time in learning to operate realistically, to be patient without any cynicism, and even — after the most disappointing failure — to execute a confident and lively come-back. As for the well-being of the citizens themselves, or more justice for the unfortunate, these questions only become part of their real priorities when they come to realize that a certain improvement in these matters is necessary for them to keep their position, and also to enjoy the "perfectly legitimate" satisfaction of knowing that they are the most skillful, the most efficient *leaders of men*.

It isn't that all these political leaders, and politicians, never have the slightest concern for the well-being of the citizens, or that they remain indifferent to the many who are the victims of all sorts of unjust behavior. It would no doubt be unfair to think so. On the other hand, it would certainly be naive to assume that none of them are ever indifferent (even voluntarily so) to the fate of any citizen or group of citizens... At any rate, all of them are certainly convinced of at least one thing: whichever policies they might choose, whichever means they might take to enforce and realize them, and whichever attitudes they might also personally adopt towards each and every one of the citizens, it would be *totally impossible* that no citizens ever suffered any disadvantages at all (even serious ones), or any unjust incidents, as a result of these coercive policies. As a matter of fact, it is often this "realistic" conviction which enables them not to worry "too much" about the painful or even unjust "repercussions", on the lives of many citizens, of policies capable of satisfying, at most, a certain majority. At least for a start...

Why say "for a start"? Simply because they know that to become great leaders of men, they must first occupy this *visible* position of "supreme" power, and then, of course, hold on to it. But to hold on to it, they must have the means to do so. In the absence of a fairly general consent, they at least need to have the minimum of required power, and above all — in order to avoid a continual use of this power —, they must be able to count on the *fear* it can really inspire and maintain. If the visible majority is actually stronger than the collection of all visible minorities (always ready to act whenever dissatisfied), then surely it is this more or less changing and impatient majority which the political rulers, and the politicians, would have to try *above all* to satisfy. But if this majority is not that strong, then it is this or that particular minority (more or less visible, yet powerful enough, by itself, to overthrow the government if it so desired), which they would *first* have to satisfy, or otherwise any particularly vigorous *group* of visible and clamoring minorities.

Once the members of a government *believed* they had made sure they would remain in position, only then could they wish to pursue *to the very end* the challenge of becoming successful leaders of men, and for *that* reason start worrying about satisfying the majority itself, or the more restless minorities — and perhaps even the most helpless of the citizens? —, with regard to their well-being or to justice itself. For these are, in fact, the main preoccupations of the great majority of citizens, the ones that arise so easily, and so aggressively, in the midst of their social relations. Whichever might be the personal concern of the political rulers and of politicians in general, regarding these matters — if they had any! —, one thing is sure: they could *not* be successful at all in pursuing their distinctive challenge, if they didn't turn themselves into skillful "social engineers", capable of grappling with the visible *and* the occult forces that constantly arise from these two main preoccupations *of the citizens themselves*. They would have to sense these forces, make way for them or else channel them, block some others (or the same ones, in other circumstances), while providing them, each time, with some kind of genuine outlet. And they would have to do all of this after having assured themselves of the help or the cooperation required for the realization of their own gigantic challenge.

If ever political rulers had their own definite conceptions of the "really" happy life and of a "true" justice, and hoped to succeed, some day, in having these conceptions acknowledged and accepted by the whole of society, they would certainly have to act very often in ways that are *contrary* to these conceptions (if they hadn't lost them somewhere along the line!), simply to *maintain* their special position. But this means that they couldn't possibly avoid becoming engineers "with dirty hands", and having to ask themselves if they should still want to become such *efficient* leaders of men, even at this rather disturbing price.

Of course, some could be driven to take on this challenge by *other* motives, perhaps more difficult to admit. For example, one could have felt a persistent longing for revenge; or the desire to elevate himself, or herself, clearly above all the others. (Here again, it would be unjust to ascribe such motives to this or that individual, but quite naive, on the other hand, to think that none of our political rulers, or politicians, are ever driven by this sort of motive.) There is also the politician who would want to prove to himself, or to certain others, that he possesses a greater personal value than that of any member of the group he was happy to belong to in the past, but who had suddenly ceased to appreciate him according to his "true" value (and had even rejected him in the "most unjust manner")...

Other real cases are common enough. In every one of our affluent societies, there is this young man who had often dreamed of becoming general manager of a very important firm. In fact, he had rapidly and brilliantly succeeded in climbing a fair number of steps towards this higher position, but his career was finally brought to a standstill by a growing series of shortcomings he just couldn't bring himself to admit, as also by the intringues of too many jealous colleagues. Those who knew him well could sadly understand his feelings of resentment, and how, for instance, he could blare out his sympathy towards "all those workers" who are the victims of "innumerable and intolerable" acts of injustice, and who are "unashamedly" scorned by the rich and by all those "vile" financial magnates. They weren't surprised, either, by the fact that he had decided to "enlighten" these workers, to make them aware of "their" dignity, and to set them against all those "most unjust" employers and bosses.

As could have been expected, the young man would also pounce on every opportunity to pass on his resentment to the poor, and the "castoff", and above all to persuade them that "together, we will *get* them!". (But what he actually meant was, more precisely:"*I* will get them!") Had he entered into politics — as he had imagined he would, for a while —, it would only have been as a way to take on this new challenge of becoming a highly appreciated leader of men — but a "social-minded" one, and more exactly, one who would have been *against* all those "unbearable" capitalists, "so disgustingly unjust and arrogant". And what about the well-being of the workers *themselves*? Or justice for *all*? —"Yes, yes of course! That is, if possible at the same time!".

Another common reason why many individuals do decide to take on the challenge of politics is their vital hope to escape, at last, from the debilitating *anonymity* to which they often think they were condemned by their poor performances at school, at college, or at the university. Rather than seeing themselves become (or remain) a *mediocre* lawyer, sociologist, engineer, manager, or bureaucrat — as compared to what they simply "know" they certainly *deserve* to become —, and well aware of their power to get people enthusiastic about causes to which they also know how to give a very "promising" appeal, they much more prefer to devote themselves to politics, a job which they nevertheless continue to despise *in itself*. But their preference is mostly that they should become known and recognized at all costs. Or that they should make the headlines at least about *something*. And so much the better if, in addition, they may also contribute to a little more justice in society, or to an increase in the well-being of "the people", that "miserably *anonymous* mass". (But they don't really require *that* much!...)

Perhaps I should insist again, at this point, on the fact that it would be unjust to name individuals in the present context, but that it would certainly be unwise to think that none of our politicians are ever motivated by similar reasons, or have such a lack of interest in the fate of the citizens *themselves*.

Even if all political rulers did want to keep their position only for self-centered reasons, it would still remain true that societies would not necessarily be worse off because of that. After all, "leaders of men" just cannot avoid *wanting* to please an ever greater number of citizens, sometimes cynically, yet as best and as decisively as they can. In fact, the greatest difficulties in having a "good" government come from somewhere else, that is, from ideological or ethical clashes between the citizens themselves.

The liberal and the socialist beliefs

Having examined the two main expectations of the citizens concerning their government, plus a certain number of obstacles that can keep governments from fulfilling these expectations, one should now consider a further difficulty, that of a *disagreement* over the question of giving priority to the liberty of the citizens, or to their well-being. On this matter, two beliefs (moral, or purely practical) are indeed opposed to each other among the politicians, as well as among the citizens themselves: the liberal and the socialist beliefs. One may notice that in societies where a greater number of citizens are rich or pretty much at ease, the liberal belief is more often the dominant one, whereas in countries where the poor and the destitute form the majority, the socialist belief can acquire a much greater expansion, and even be shared by many of the citizens who are living a very decent life.

The liberal belief highly values, of course, the freedom of the individual, regarding it as one of the goods to which everyone, as a rule, has a permanent right. But that is perhaps only because this particular good seems necessary for the acquisition (and the enjoyment) of an even more important good, namely, "the happy life". For liberals in general, it is simply impossible that justice could ever threaten anyone's well-being, except "to a small degree", or "within certain limits". For example, if some of the poor really suffered, or suffered "too much", then the richer citizens would certainly have the *obligation* to help them — perhaps even as a matter of *justice* —, but provided always that this help would not cause "too great" a harm to *their own* well-being. (As a rule, no government would have the right to *force* the rich to help the poor, because of the risk that the government itself, in so doing, would cause "too serious" a harm to the well-being of the rich, and thus violate *their* right to liberty.)

The best way for the rich to help the poor would then be to acquire more and more liberty for themselves, this liberty enabling them to become even wealthier and happier, while their freely undertaken enterprises provided more jobs for the poor — who would in turn become more and more wealthy themselves, and so on... Indeed, the more wealthy the rich become, the more able they are to provide the less resourceful citizens with *indirect* help (without putting their own well-being at too great a risk), and the more they are inclined to help them even directly, at times, and without feeling obliged to do so (as they would, if it were a matter of justice or fairness).

The liberal belief seems to derive from common sense itself. Would it be reasonable, indeed, for the sick, the crippled, the unfit, the unintelligent or the unlucky people, to expect, as a matter of *justice*, that others gave up a happier life in order to *really* help them? Could justice reasonably demand things which, if they were to be *adequately* done, could no doubt create situations where the less happy would then live a *slightly* happier life (but not a really happy one!), while the happier citizens could very well become *less* happy? Could the poor — or a government — reasonably demand that the rich start living a less interesting life, or perhaps even a dull one, simply because the lives of other citizens are constantly subjected to ill fortune? (Wouldn't the poor themselves be the unjust or the unfair ones, if they expected such a generosity — such an *adequate* aid — from the rich?) Besides, one should be a little more realistic (or so it would seem), for even if the rich agreed to deprive themselves of some of their time, money, and leisure, so as to provide a *real* help for the poor, the latter are so numerous — and often so incapable — that the day could never come when *all* human beings (the former rich as well as the former poor) could at last live a truly happy life.

Nevertheless, it must be very difficult, at times, even for the more hardened liberals, to declare, without any afterthoughts, that all that the underpriviledged would have to do is to "wisen up, get a move on, or else be patient until their luck finally came", since it is a fact (isn't it?) that "those who are healthy and fit cannot be expected to start living a diminished life, so that a few misfits (or 'free riders'?) might live just a little better"... Liberal believers often seem to take fairness into account only when members of their crowd are concerned, that is, people who, like themselves, would be more interested in their own well-being and liberty than in other *persons*, even among the wealthy ones.

The *socialist* belief, on the other hand, is apparently more sensitive to the fate of the unfortunate, of the people they consider not so much as being sick or unlucky, but rather as having been *oppressed*. It isn't that such a belief values justice *itself*, which would then be what it urged its followers above all to restore. More immediately, the socialists simply cannot bear the sight of all these miserable people who were deprived of a minimum of well-being, of the little bit of happiness that they had (or could have had), by those who, for their own benefit, had taken possession of the natural resources and the means of production. The fact that certain minorities, in the past, had or had not done something totally unjust in monopolizing everything, that fact, in itself, doesn't seem to worry the socialists. They are actually more preoccupied by the prospects of a happier life for the helpless and the destitute, for all those who suffer (or "should" suffer?) from the fact that others (or "the system"?) make it impossible for them to live a better life, as well as a happier one. What the socialist belief can hardly tolerate is not so much injustice itself, as the sight of these bruised and impaired lives, the consequences of a "nauseating" coercion. (Incidentally, the word "justice" doesn't often appear in the discourses and writings of the more communist-minded socialists, who apparently were not even interested in finding an equivalent for this "bourgeois" notion.)

The socialists living in our democratic countries do have a certain concern for the liberty of *every* citizen, even when they have trouble finding the political means to *really* help the underpriviledged. But as the difficulties increase, their belief strongly inclines them to sacrifice the liberty or the well-being of the rich, in favor of a better life for the unfortunate and the poor. And this time, in the name of justice, that is, of the *rights* of the latter. Just as in the liberal belief, where the liberty and the well-being of the rich prevail over those of the disabled and the poor, so do liberty and well-being prevail in the socialist belief; but in this case, the losers are the well-provided and the rich. The socialist believer is convinced that it would not be "reasonable" (and would *therefore* be unjust?) if the rich continued to live such an easy and pleasant life, while many underpriviledged and helpless citizens are inexcusably in need of a minimum of well-being, or of a life which would be at least sometimes happy.

Such a believer is understandably inclined to want to dispossess the rich, while perhaps pointing out to them that their personal resources — but *not* their offensive luxury — is all they really needed to live as happily as before; and that if not, "then all they would have to do is to start raising or finding a new fortune, since they all seem so very good at *that*!". In any case, to dispossess the rich, in this manner, would only be *justice*, the underpriviledged having a *right* to this aid, to this "retribution", or better: to this "redressing of the situation".

And yet, there must surely be moments when the socialist believer would hesitate before deciding to be so categorical and harsh with all the richer citizens. Is it true that if "those exploiters of the weak" declared themselves unable to supply a really *efficient* aid for the poor, then they would certainly deserve the contempt which such a phrase seems to express? That is to say, a contempt coming from the socialist believers themselves, and which could be just as *objectionable* as the contempt for the poor that all these "exploiters" are accused of having? It would seem that the socialists are more often concerned with the well-being of the helpless, or with the "redressing" of the situation, than with the persons *themselves* — the persons of the rich, or even the persons of the unfortunate, whose liberation they most certainly wish, but perhaps much more for their own gratification...

Since both the liberal and the socialist beliefs are present in all our densely populated societies, governments cannot avoid feeling the pressure of conflicting expectations. Liberal believers object to most government policies, which they consider as interfering with the citizens' freedom of movement, of enterprise, and even of choice (in the conduct of their lives). They accuse the government of unjust coercion, of "totalitarianism", every time it oversteps the limited role of "night-watchman". (In their minds, this role is clearly limited to protection against violence, theft, and breaches of contract.) On the other hand, socialist believers keep urging the government to *force* the well-provided citizens, by means of laws that are ever more efficient (and therefore just?), to refrain from exploiting or oppressing the more helpless citizens, and even to make up for their unjust behavior of the past, by contributing to their welfare and liberation.

Is it really possible for a government to be at all efficient in accomplishing its task — whichever it may be! — under the pressure of these expectations of the liberal and the socialist believers? What can a government reasonably hope to accomplish for the whole of society, in circumstances of this nature? Could it be that a government's power to coerce were but one social force among others, often more impressive, but such that no one could possibly foresee whether its effects would in fact be appreciated, or totally condemned?

Are the projects and expectations realistic?

Very few citizens would think it really preferable to leave all individuals free to act as they wished. In any case, *not* at all times, and *not* concerning any wish that anyone happened to have. One need only think of certain persons or types of persons, and of the frequent harms and damages which would certainly occur. Most citizens actually prefer that someone (or a group of citizens) should see to it that the people's behavior were carefully observed and then regulated, so that the more damaging acts or omissions would be clearly prohibited by law, and even enforced, as necessary, by very effective penalties.

The existence of a government possessing a force really superior to all others is thus *in principle* a most welcome thing. But haven't we already noticed how insurmountably difficult it is, for any government (even a "good" one), to accomplish its own particular task? Or how impossible it seemed to be, even for the most experienced and cautious government, not to become itself responsible for many of the enterprises that are unjust and harmful for the citizens? It still remains a fact, however, that most people consider governments, although never competent enough, as something that is certainly worth having, at least as "a lesser evil", if not as a necessary one.

One can always ask if even a "good" government is really the *lesser* evil. Is it true that having no government at all would necessarily mean greater harms, as well as an increase in the number of acts of injustice? Many have had serious doubts about that — and not only among the anarchists or the most hardened libertarians. If the particular expectations of many citizens concerning their government are so often frustrated, and if the political rulers see so many of their projects simply disintegrate (or else cause harms that are contrary to their intent), could the reason be that these particular expectations and projects are not really the ones which would correspond to the *actual* needs of the citizens, and especially not to the more demanding of their deeper aspirations?

This question — this hypothesis — may have been suggested by the presence, within our conceptions of what would be unjust, of a widespread *presupposition*, one which has not been noticed very often, and was therefore never closely examined or really called in question.

It seems, indeed, that everyone is convinced of *knowing* what is unjust, and what a "serious" harm, or damage, would be. (At any rate, people often behave as if they seldom had any doubts about these matters.) It is certainly true that people very often know that what they themselves would like to do at this moment would be unjust to another person. But they are also convinced of knowing *just as well* that what they now *see* someone doing to someone else (or to them) is certainly unjust. Or at least a "very serious" harm. It is precisely this misleading presupposition that will have to be examined in the following sections. It should then become clear that if ever one could know which behavior, which activity, or which observable event is definitely unjust (or would at least cause a grave damage), then one could not have come to know this fact *only* by having looked at the behavior, the activity, or the event in question, or by having been able to anticipate their consequences — as if it were possible to see, *in these facts alone*, what it is that would make them at this moment unjust, or very seriously harmful. (And this applies even to acts "so obviously unjust", or "damaging", as the ones we call murder, rape, torture, and so on.)

A careful examination of the *reasons* we commonly advance to convince others that such and such a thing is unjust or not, or is definitely harmful or not: such an examination — coming in the next section — should bring out at least two important points. First, we would certainly be acting unjustly in doing such and such a thing, if we thought ourselves unable to do the thing in question, at this moment, *without* any contempt — any *freely adopted* contempt — towards other persons. (This particular kind of contempt will no doubt have to be carefully described.) Secondly, the harms or losses caused to someone would be "really serious" — and not just painful —, if we believed that because of them, the person involved might become *permanently unable* to live a "fundamentally" happy life.

Such will appear to be, then, our more spontaneous conceptions of the just and the unjust, and of "really serious" harms. They are conceptions of *what it is*, about an act, that *makes it* an act of injustice; or what it is, about a harm, that makes it a "serious" one.

If this elucidation of our reasons should turn out to be correct, we would then have to admit that no one *knows*, in most cases, which particular harm would be a serious one for himself or herself, or for anyone else. And we would also have to concede that even though everyone could very often know if he or she would be doing something unjust in choosing to do this or that particular thing, yet in most cases no one could know if *the others* were acting unjustly, right now. Does that mean, then, that no government (or no individual) would have the *right* to keep citizens from producing acts of injustice, or causing harms to others, since they couldn't really be *sure* if these acts of the citizens were acts of injustice, or if the harms were really serious? In the next section, it will become clear that the answer to this question is: "not necessarily", since there *does* exist a practical criterion capable of indicating when, in which circumstances, and even why a government (or an individual) could cause harms or difficulties to others, *without* thereby producing acts of injustice, or causing "serious" damages. (One may already expect that people often do, in fact, apply such a criterion, even if many of them are not always actually aware of it.)

Once everyone's *implicit* conceptions of justice and of serious damages were clearly perceived, it would seem that many of the more immediate expectations of the citizens, concerning their government, would have to be modified. In some cases quite substantially, but always with a view to having them become more realistic. The same would also apply to the projects and policies of the political rulers: the desire to fulfill the reasonable expectations of the citizens could no longer have, as its *main* object, the simultaneous (and anyhow impossible) satisfaction of the more immediate desires of all the citizens; nor the disappearance of all the damages and difficulties that some citizens inflict on others; nor the elimination, by sheer force, of all the "unjust" acts that the political rulers (with a majority of citizens) had defined according to what struck them as being the most harmful or most revolting human behavior. (But first of all, the *changing* character of the connections between the particular harms inflicted on others, and injustice itself, would have to be more clearly perceived.)

Even if the expectations of the citizens did become more realistic, thus allowing the projects of the rulers to become more realizable, one could still predict that the problems of life in society would not be solved for all that. Indeed, not all citizens would then wish to limit themselves to these more reasonable expectations (or would be able to do so). Likewise, not all political rulers would want to limit their projects to the fulfilment of these more realistic expectations, or would in fact be able to do that. Furthermore, there is even reason to believe that, on the whole, things cannot but remain pretty much as they are...

So what is there to think, or to hope, then, for the citizens, the politicians, and the rulers who would like to keep on being realists, while remaining *effectively* sensitive to the hardships of so many citizens, and to the more demanding aspirations of *all* the citizens? Are there enterprises, or activities, which everyone could take up for his or her own benefit, as well as for that of the others, while maintaining a more or less "utopian" concern for justice *and* a fundamentally happy life for everyone? That is the question which will again have to be tackled, in the last section of this study; but perhaps, then, with the help of more appropriate means.

2. INJUSTICE AND CONTEMPT

Governments usually claim they have not only the power to impose laws on the citizens, and of course to enforce those laws, but also the *right* to exercise such a power. Certainly, at least, when the laws and enforcement are meant to prevent acts of *injustice*, or to restore justice itself. Even though some specialists and many citizens doubt that any government, as such, could have this right, yet most people consider that as a rather obvious fact, since one of the things they expect from their government is precisely that it maintained and restored justice. But there are frequent and serious disagreements among them, especially over the question of *which* particular behavior would certainly be unjust, and in *which* circumstances. (Only think, for example, of nuclear warfare, capital punishment, abortion, and mercy-killing.)

Because of the number and variety of opinions concerning just and unjust behavior, many citizens have become dogmatic, that is, compelled to think that "the *others*" are outright liars, or else totally mistaken. ("A behavior is just, or it isn't. But this particular behavior is obviously unjust. Therefore, all those 'others' who pretend it is *not* unjust are either hypocrites, or plainly mistaken.") Other citizens have become skeptics instead, or relativists who would rather believe that there are as many kinds of unjust acts as there are subjective conceptions of what is unjust — which is the equivalent of believing that no one could know *which* concrete behavior is really, or "objectively", unjust. (Of course, most skeptics find it difficult to maintain that attitude in everyday life, especially when they happen to witness acts that are "unbearably" unjust...) One can suspect that both of these beliefs are in some ways faulty, but that each one of them could still be the expression of a significant part of our experiences and conception of injustice.

Before starting to examine the question of whether or not a government has, or *could* have, a particular right to use *force* in trying to prevent unjust behavior — especially when uncommonly harmful —, it would certainly be helpful to find out, then, if most citizens wouldn't have, after all, a fairly universal conception of what an unjust behavior would be. Contrary to what the impatience of the dogmatic people, or the weariness of the skeptics could have led them to believe, it will become clear, in the immediately following pages, that the citizens might actually *have* such a conception.

Is coercion always unjust?

One of the most widely acknowledged acts of injustice is, without any doubt, the one which consists in making others endure things they simply wouldn't want to endure. Or things which could only be perceived by them as damages, or definite annoyances. But that which constitutes more precisely an act of injustice is not so much the fact that others are forced to suffer more or less painful experiences, as the fact that they are made to suffer something (anything at all) *against* their wishes, or *against* their own will. It is also true, however, that a person is not at all considered as being unjust, for example, when compelling a thief (surely against his will!) to let go of his spoils. It is commonly believed, in fact, that coercion is not unjust, when used to keep others from doing *themselves* something unjust.

Now if all *other* constraints are to be considered unjust, how can we know, for sure, whether or not the coercion we are now using (to keep someone else from doing something unjust) does not in fact *exceed*, in intensity or duration, the one which would have been quite sufficient? (And whether or not, therefore, we would *ourselves* be unjust to this other person?) How is one to know, in the first place, if what this other person is doing must certainly be unjust? Let us then examine the case more closely, by means of the following sketches.

Here is a brawny, rough-looking youngster, fourteen years old, brutalizing a little old lady. Do I have the right to stop him, if I know that the police wouldn't come round till much later, and if I have already warned him to quit, but only to be told to mind my own damn business? Would I be unjust if I forced him to quit being so brutal, while knowing very well that this old lady keeps spreading all sorts of slanderous stories about the boy's father? (Wouldn't that be helping her to avoid getting what she deserves in all justice?...) But what if, on the other hand, the young bully hated both the old lady *and* his own father? Or if I were fairly sure that later on, his revenge would be all the more brutal, and that the police could not possibly guarantee that his prey would always be protected? Or if I doubted that my own threats could actually persuade the young fellow to abandon his purpose? But in the presence of such a brutal behavior, couldn't it also be the case that I had not only the right, but even the *obligation* to force the young bully to let go of the old lady, my obligation being precisely what gave me that particular right? (In this case, the right would be the one that I would have the obligation, in all fairness, *not* to renounce.)

Let us imagine, more specifically, that the young "bully" manages to explain that he only wants to punish "the old bitch", not too severely, yet enough to force her to really quit making his father relapse into serious depressions. Hearing this, the old lady quickly yells out that he's lying, that he's exaggerating, but that anyway she will never again even *talk* to anyone about his father. But the young fellow insists that I mustn't believe her, that she's a sly old fox, and that he absolutely has to terrify her, if he wants her to lose all desire to carry on with her poisonous gossip. I try to draw his attention to the police and the courts, but simply cannot convince him: his reply is that the judges won't believe him (he has a police record of a couple of small thefts), and besides, the old witch has the incredible power of winning over the pity of anyone who doesn't know her as well as *he* does... During the discussion, he keeps on jabbing the old lady, sometimes shouting at her that she will certainly remember this moment and never *dare* open her mouth any more.

What should I decide, at this point? Do I still have the obligation, or even the *right* to stop the young man from being so brutal? Is he actually brutal, seeing how so unbelievably callous the old lady seems to be? Do I have the obligation, or at least the right to stop him from using such means, if there seems to be no other way to protect his father's mental health? On the other hand, is it always true, in fact, that no one has the right to take justice in his or her own hands, unless something more unjust, or more revolting, were to follow?

There is a further question. Would I have the right to force the young fellow to quit (against his will), if I noticed along the way that to succeed, I would myself have to brutalize him? (There is quite a bit of blood over his face already, but surely I must be allowed to protect myself a little?) And if I were persuaded, up to now, that he certainly had no right to hit the old lady to hard (supposedly just to be *efficient*!), wouldn't I, too, be unjust if I hit him as forcefully as I thought were needed for him to *really* move off, that is, to renounce *all* future use of violence against the old lady?

One may of course point out that not all solutions have been considered, or that the difficulty itself comes from the fact that obvious possibilities have been neglected. For example, shouldn't I simply drag these two people along, up to the nearest police station? Or be content with holding on to the young man until a police car came cruising by, or until witnesses appeared and went to phone the police in my place? But if I just cannot see how the police itself could keep the young man from finally trapping the old lady, couldn't I myself decide to watch over her and assure her protection? Or discuss with her the possibilities of moving to another part of the city? And so on? Now that would take a lot of time, wouldn't it? Aren't all these assumptions totally incompatible with my other obligations, my family obligations, my social and my professional obligations? (Come to think of it, I am *already* very late!)

Which, then, would be the exact right, or the particular obligation I would actually have, at this moment? And concerning *whom*? And referring to *which* degree of "efficiency"? In other words, which decision, coming from me, would be just, unjust, or indifferent, at the *present* moment? [2]

---

[2] When dealing with just or unjust acts, choices, or behavior — and with rights, obligations, or values —, this study refers, in most cases, to the *moral* character of all these, and even to their *natural* moral character. Furthermore, the word 'moral' will apply only to cases in which people have the capacity to *freely* choose to act, or not to act. (For only then could any act or omission be considered *morally* just or unjust, and any right or obligation a *moral* one.)

An act is 'naturally' unjust means only that it is unjust not because people have *freely* decided (independently of each other or by common agreement) that it would be so, but because people have the feeling, or the conviction, that it *already is* unjust, or that it *would* be if they actually produced

Do I ever have the right, then, to constrain anyone? Can I ever be obliged, in all fairness, to force other people? If I am at all careful and perceptive, the question could finally come down to this one: is it possible for me to have the right (or even the obligation) to coerce anyone, when I really don't know *who* is at fault, or who is unjust; or *what* force (physical or psychological) would be neither too great, nor insufficient anyway; or *what* the more remote consequences would be? Could the "pacifists" be right, after all, in the majority of cases? (But if so, how is one to *know* if this particular case belongs to that majority, or is a doubtful and therefore negligible exception?)

Many people seem to think that to bring up such questions, or to make up sketches that are "so intricate and dramatic", is to take pleasure in seeing morals — and life itself — as something terribly complicated. These people are convinced that, in themselves, life and morality — if the latter is not just a delusion! — must be a lot more simple than all that. (That is of course true, ...in a sense.) For them, the ambiguity of our desires, and the excessive need to justify everything, is what induces researchers and professors to complicate life and morals — in fact, to distort them. Well, perhaps. But then perhaps the reason why, for example, the questions and sketches that have just been presented might seem so involved, and so unjustifiably removed from the actual life of "normal" people, could simply be that these people happen to have "a nice quiet and easy temperament". For it does sometimes appear, in fact, that in order to penetrate to a certain depth in questions of social justice (or of morality in general), one would have to feel, in one's own core, some of the more demanding, the more resentful, or the more "unwholesome" human desires, as well as some of the more serene or the more intense human aspirations —as many people, in all spheres of society, actually do.

The conditions for injustice

Despite the difficulty of identifying and accurately describing all the significant components of any act of injustice, it does seem quite obvious that the

---

it. When referring to natural rights or obligations, the word 'natural' *only* means, here, that their existence is ultimately independent of any human choice or decision.

number of such acts, committed in our world, is impressively high. Influential people, governments, majorities, and many individuals do all sorts of unjust things, in order to attain their ends. But are these judgments true? Are they adequately based on our common experiences of unjust behavior? Perhaps not too adequately, as I would now like to show.

A first series of observations and questions should allow anyone to become more aware of what we commonly require, as necessary components, for an act to be counted as truly unjust. For example, could there be such a thing as the "unjust" behavior of floods, earthquakes, or famines? Or of a heart attack, a cancer, a mad dog, or the slow dying away of a loved person? Do I really have *rights* concerning the behavior of these beings or events, rights that they would therefore have to respect, or otherwise be unjust to me? No one seriously thinks that the river, in overflowing and sweeping away my house, has been unjust; or that my cancerous cells, or the dog who bit me, were unjust. I wouldn't even think of claiming my rights from the illness (or the impending death) of a loved one; or from the sun's unbearable heat. I would say, at the most, that "*it* is" unjust, or unfair, *that* such things should happen to me or to others, but certainly not that these things or events have *themselves* done something unjust. It could happen, in some of these cases, that people would feel themselves the victims of an "unjust" event, but without there being any really competent or adequate "wrongdoer". (Unless, in a rather mysterious way, the "wrongdoer" were life itself, or "existence", or what they might call their own "destiny". But they would probably concede that they were then using some form of spontaneous *personification...*)

It would also be impossible for me to think that I had the right not to be *accidentally* injured by strangers, or even by friends or acquaintances. If any of these persons had injured or inconvenienced me to any degree, but not at all *on purpose* — not having willfully wished or allowed that to happen —, then I would certainly think they had done absolutely nothing unjust. And if I thought that these accidents had actually reduced my chances for a happy future, I would perhaps consider myself the victim, in a sense, of "unjust" events, but only "through" these people, there having been no other "instigators" of these events than "life", or "existence in general", or my own "destiny". But how could I then believe that *these* "producers" of "unjust" events had acted on purpose, and had *really* focused on me?

Or that it was only by accident — yet quite certainly and "objectively" — that they had acted against my rights? Could I really believe that they were *obliged* to respect my rights, perhaps in having made me a certain promise? If not, then was it my own desire of justice, or of a happy life, that had "promised" me something?... So where, then, does the injustice of unjust events finally come from? Are there even unjust events, anywhere at all?

To be considered as "acting" against my rights (or as "doing" something unjust), it seems that a violently overflowing river, or an earthquake, or a vicious dog, would have to *be conscious* of the rights I have (and of their obligation to respect them), and also choose *by themselves* (or freely) to act against those rights. Furthermore, all these things and events (including "existence in general", or "my own destiny") would even have to be aware of me — or so it seems —, that is, aware of the fact that those rights are *mine*, and that they therefore have an obligation concerning *me*. Without this particular awareness, they would perhaps be doing something unjust, but certainly not "against" me, or to *me*. (But where would the "victim" be, if it were true that something *unjust* really did happen?)

Because of their total lack of the required awareness, things and events like heat waves, earthquakes, tornadoes, floods, diseases, dangerous animals, and eventually "existence" itself, or my own "destiny", could never make me the victim of any *unjust* "behavior". I can always cry out from under the blows dealt by any of these things or events, and even shout my indignation at them, if that could somehow alleviate my pain; but none of them has ever even thought of me, or had anything at all against me, and *could*, therefore, have been unjust to me, or to any other person or thing. (Unless, of course, I absolutely had to personify something, *anything*...)

Can we be so sure that the situation is very *different*, when the causes of supposedly unjust events are human beings? Unlike hurricanes and vicious animals, persons can often be aware of causing harms to others; they often feel the *obligation* not to do things that would hurt them, and they are also convinced, in such cases, of being able to choose between acting in accordance with this obligation, *or* against it. Should I say, then, that I am the victim of unjust behavior if my employer fires me, while "explaining" that he really can't help it, that I am the unfortunate victim of "budget restrictions"? Is *he* the one who is causing the harm, or is it more exactly his boss? Or the latest vote of the shareholders? Or the government's most recent law?

Why is it that the river is not unjust to me, or to anyone else, in carrying away my house and drowning my whole family? It is no doubt because the river has no choice at all between being or not being harmful — much less unjust — to anyone. But then why is the person who, out of jealousy, causes me to suffer all sorts of unpleasant things: why is this person *unjust* to me? Can I be *sure* that this person isn't just a river "overflowing with jealousy", instead of one who — as my reactions imply — really does have a choice between wanting and not wanting me to suffer these irritating things? And if I am aware of *not* being so sure whether this person is or is not such a "river", and yet let myself decide that he or she is in fact unjust, am *I* then unjust to him or to her?

On the other hand, how would I have to judge my own attitude if, besides having noticed that I am not sure about all that, I were nevertheless convinced of having the choice between considering that person unjust, *or* not passing any judgment at all about him or her, and then chose *anyway* to let myself consider that person unjust?... If ever I were to be definitely unjust to anyone, wouldn't it be precisely in a case like this one? Could it be, however, that neither I, nor that person, were unjust, both of us having behaved like "overflowing rivers", and no more unjustly, therefore, than two wolves lashing at each other; or like a pack of young hoodlums who, whether or not under the influence of drugs, keep spreading terror in the subways? Being aware of causing harms to others — and of the obligation not to behave that way — is certainly not enough: to be unjust, one need also have the capacity, each time, to choose and to act *freely*.

In most cases it would be impossible, then, to really know if (or when) *the others* were unjust. Certain observations tend to make us presume that they were, in fact, unjust, but we often make unnoticed *mistakes*. These would need to be detected, and then interpreted. Thus, the scorching sun or the mad dog have nothing against me, and yet, I would "almost" want to say that they *are* against me, considering the way the sun constantly "stares" at me, and how the dog is so very much "after me". Natural events, life, existence, or my own destiny, cannot possibly be after me personally; and yet, I could almost think that they actually were, the way they have been persistently "assaulting" me — more than anyone else! — during the last six months. (But no, that's impossible!)

A similar caution should also apply to human beings. For example, what should we think of this woman, this superintendent of mine, who never misses an opportunity to humiliate me, her male secretary, with her ironic smiles and her scornful remarks? Is she really against me, contemptuous of me, or is it just that it "almost" looks as if she didn't care whether she were, or were not unjust to *me*? In any case, can it be said that my superintendent has always been capable of freely *choosing* to harass or not to harass me, and to have or not to have a contemptuous attitude towards me? Could we even say that she was capable of at least *not* having a special dislike concerning me? If not, couldn't she decide to really *want* to get rid of this dislike, and of the constant urge to be contemptuous towards me? Isn't she capable of *trying*, at least, to really *want* to do that?

Perhaps not. For instance, what if she always tried to resist this urge within her, often succeeded in really wanting that, yet was hardly ever successful in restraining many contradictory feelings, words, and gestures? To top it all, what if she has always been totally unable, in spite of all her efforts, to even talk to me about that? If I ever became aware of that, would I think she was unjust? (Would I think she was unjust to *me*?) And if I did think she was still unjust and contemptible — a real bitch! —, would I myself be unjust to *her*? Or could it be, on the other hand, that *both* of us were only the helpless witnesses of two "overflowing rivers", or of the many blindly "hostile" forces of nature?

Even though the preceding questions and observations may have cast a doubt on our capacity to know if (or when) *the others* are really doing something unjust, still they have brought out some of the reasons we have, and rely on, to believe that someone has acted unjustly; and therefore, some of the *conditions* we require for an act, or a conduct, to be unjust. To recall them briefly: the agent must be *conscious* of what he or she is doing. (Hailstorms and sleepwalkers are not unjust.) Also, the agent must believe that he or she has the *obligation* not to do, to others, what he or she might be inclined to do. (A vicious dog cannot be unjust, nor perhaps a madman.) In addition, the act or the consequences must not be accidentally produced, but willfully, and *on purpose*. (One who simply cannot resist the urge to do something which will hurt someone else, is not acting unjustly.) This last condition finally implies that the agent must act *freely*, and that *only* the acts that would have been selected out of his or her own free *choice*, could be truly unjust.

Although one's awareness of this last condition is not always clear, and one's spontaneous judgments concerning unjust behavior not always consistent with it, it is nevertheless a fact that this requirement of the agent's liberty is very present in our *conception* of unjust acts and conduct. As has been shown above — but should be verified by *each* person —, the reasons we most commonly put forward to *justify* our belief that a behavior was, or was not unjust, those reasons really do imply this fundamental requirement of the liberty of the agent. But let us turn to yet another important condition.

Injustice and the person

It will now become clear that to behave *unjustly* with regard to others, one must not only be causing them some harm while having freely chosen to do so, but also be aware of the fact that through this behavior, he or she is now dealing with the person *itself* of these others.

In the present context, "the person itself" will refer to that element, in human beings, which more specifically enables them to act *freely*, and therefore differentiates them from beings that are unable to do so. (Again, in the present context, it matters very little how adequately this element could be "pictured" — if ever it could be! —, since the cognitive and substantial meaning of the word "person" should become sufficiently understood as this study is pursued.) Finally, a person will be considered here as having chosen (and acted) "freely", if — and only if — that person has made this choice exist while having been able to make it or *not* to make it exist, and was also the *one and only* being which *could* have made it exist.

The foregoing definition of a "free" choice was so formulated as to exclude the more frequent cases where someone else — or forces of all sorts — actually *coerce* people into making choices that are totally unavoidable, and therefore not strictly *their own* (as would be the really unconstrained, or "free" choices of the individuals who chose (and acted) out of their own persons *alone*).

A few observations. When wishing to keep rats or bugs from causing damages or plain annoyances, one doesn't hesitate, but simply decides to get rid of them, once and for all, by killing them. People usually don't think they are unjust to beings of that kind, when they prefer killing them instead of putting them in "prison" and trying — for as long as required — to train them not to harm anybody. On the other hand, when people wish to keep a gang of teen-age "bullies" from terrorizing their neighborhood, or simply causing trouble, this time they do hesitate. Even if they believed these bullies incorrigible, they would still be afraid of being actually unjust, if they were to have *that* "vermin" exterminated. Many people are even inclined to think that putting offenders behind bars might also be unjust, if it were for *a whole lifetime*. Most of them believe it would certainly be, if it were done without even trying to "rehabilitate", or "socialize" these persons.

What does that difference exactly mean? Why should one be *more* considerate when dealing with persons (even the more harmful or unjust), than when having to deal with animals (even the more harmless and gentle)? One doesn't ordinarily think that he or she is being unjust, when putting a canary or a hamster in a cage; yet one might feel unjust in keeping a thief behind bars longer than necessary. Why, then, should human beings be treated, in general,with more consideration, or attention, than animals?[3] If the reason is that human beings occupy a "higher" level of life, of consciousness, or of liberty, then why would one often feel unjust in causing inconveniences to persons who are severely disabled or mentally ill, or who would be totally incapable of acting freely? Is it because human beings are so sensitive that they would suffer more than any animal, in spite of certain appearances?

But if *suffering* were the reason, how is it that I could feel unjust in stealing one of my neighbor's belongings, while being convinced that even though he would never have wanted to offer that object to anyone, he would most probably think he had lost it himself, and would most certainly never suffer from the loss, nor even

[3] 'With more consideration' should not mean that animals could be treated in any way whichever — with cruelty, for example.

miss the thing at all? What is the reason, this time, for the feeling I have of being somehow unjust to this neighbor of mine?

The preceding contrasts and questions may have suggested the presence, in our *applied* conceptions of unjust behavior, of a requirement which would be the most essential component of these conceptions, and which would even help to explain their other components. According to this particular requirement, that which basically constitutes any act of injustice is *not only* — because not *always*! — the fact of causing a voluntary harm to others (or anything against their will), nor even the fact that there was a voluntary lack of "respect" for their life, their health, their will, their liberty, or their well-being. The principal component of any act of injustice is a particular *attitude*, one which is *not* towards "things" like the ones just mentioned, but towards the person itself of any individual. It is above all a refusal, that of having a minimum of consideration, respect, or concern for this person itself.

To be unjust to others, it isn't enough that one happened to *feel* no respect (or to *feel* a strong contempt) for the behavior or the character of these people, or for their incapacities, flaws, or unpleasant defects. More to the point, one must *freely* choose to have no consideration or respect for their persons themselves. When freely chosen, this lack of consideration would not be a purely "negative" attitude, but a truly personal one, that is, an attitude of personal *contempt* towards the persons involved.(The meaning of the word "contempt", as that of the word "consideration", will of course have to be carefully defined, in section 4.)

If this freely chosen absence of consideration actually *is* the necessary as also the sufficient condition for a person to be unjust to others, one could easily understand why, then, the latter need not be *aware* of being such "victims". More often than not, and in spite of the appearances, victims *could not* be aware of that, since they cannot be sure that the people who have harmed them, even deliberately, were in fact capable of a *freely* chosen contempt concerning their own persons. For the same reason, one can also understand why persons can be unjust — as they in fact *feel* that they are — to someone who is not only absent, but even happens to have died without their having been informed. In such cases, simply thinking of a particular individual is an occasion for them to freely refuse to have any consideration for "persons in general".

To be able to behave unjustly, then, people need not be in the presence of persons who are adults, awake, sane, and capable here and now of acting freely. All that is necessary *in fact* is that they *believed* that "something like a person" is here concerned, or that they themselves behaved, with regard to "whatever" is concerned, as they would if they were absolutely sure they were dealing with a true person. So it is, for example, that someone could very well be acting unjustly with regard to "persons in general", if he or she were shouting spiteful insults at life, at existence itself, or at "the totality of events" — while knowing that these couldn't possibly be unjust to anyone, nor even be aware of the contempt anyone could have for them. That would more certainly be the case, of course, if that person strongly wished that all these "things" *could* become sensitive to the personal contempt which he or she really wanted to have towards "them".

The same thing could also happen if a young man couldn't help *doubting* whether this foetus (or his "vegetative" old father) were already (or still) a person, while continuing to think — rightly or not — that the risk would probably be "too great" of not having enough consideration for these "potential" persons, if he decided to *go ahead* with what he wanted to do. Perhaps this young man freely chose to be lacking in consideration "anyway", or to let himself have an unjust attitude, at least regarding "persons in general". But maybe not, since he might have been able to decide the very same thing while *freely* choosing to maintain (or even to renew) all of his consideration towards "persons in general", including these doubtful ones. Only this young man himself could really know, of course, if he chose to be unjust or not, even if he remained unsure whether he was immediately dealing with definite persons, or only with "vegetative" beings.

Although the *only* unjust acts would be the ones which consisted in freely choosing to have no consideration (or to have contempt) towards other persons, that doesn't mean that no other behavior or activity could be unjust. On the contrary, any behavior can become unjust when it is part of the *concrete* unfolding or extension, in the world, of someone's freely chosen contempt towards other persons. That can happen, for instance, when a particular activity is the expression or manifestation of such a contempt; or when a behavior is simply its physical or psychological outgrowth. But these most frequent cases simply stress the fact that, taken as they are *in themselves only*, no behavior, activity, or attitude (other than freely chosen contempt) is ever unjust, although all of them can often be considered as participating, to a certain extent, in the unjust character of someone's contempt.

If this kind of contempt is, in fact, the only possible act of true injustice, then the only *right* that persons could actually have would be the right *not* to be made objects of a freely adopted contempt. But in practice, this turns out to be a right to the freely chosen *consideration* of all the other persons, since the only way someone could actually succeed in freely choosing *not* to have a contemptuous attitude towards another person, would be to choose to have a really personal consideration towards this other person itself. For the same practical reason, persons may also have the right to many other attitudes or "dispositions" of the others — like sincere sympathy, encouraging words, a concrete aid, congratulations, even if these others thought they didn't seem to "deserve" such gestures —; but that would concern only those who, in certain cases, could not possibly choose to have a minimum of consideration for these persons themselves *without* choosing, at the same time, to try to adopt these other attitudes and activities.

A relativistic criterion?

Our more common everyday behavior and beliefs seem to imply, then, that in order to really *know* if abortion, mercy-killing, rape, support of war, lying, "using" the helpless, violence and seduction are unjust — even *before* knowing if government laws, or a social consensus, have already prohibited these acts —, one would have to know, in each case, whether he or she would be capable of doing these things *without* freely choosing, at the same time, to be personally *contemptuous* towards other persons. If someone is sincerely convinced of having this capability right now, then he or she would not be unjust in doing the thing in question. On the contrary, he or she would actually have the natural right, at this moment, to do that thing. (The word "natural" only means, here, that the right is one whose existence, in a person's conviction, is not the result of the *free* choice or decision on any human being. In the same sense, there are also many "natural" moral obligations, laws and values.)

If, on the other hand, a person has to admit that he or she does *not* have this capability right now, then of course doing the things concerned would be acting unjustly. (And he or she would know that, and would now be forced to decide.) We therefore have, here, a natural criterion for just or unjust acts and behavior, which we might call the "contempt-criterion". Any person may apply it to his or her own case, in all circumstances, even though it doesn't enable anyone to avoid, each time, the painful or tragic doubts which may precede or accompany the actual choice of one's own motives.

Now why would it seem to be so difficult, both in theory and in practice, to acknowledge the fact that "contempt" is the one and only criterion for all unjust acts and behavior? One of the reasons is no doubt the following. Since this criterion never informs anyone as to whether or not *the others* are doing something unjust when causing harms to certain persons, or when acting against widely accepted laws, many people tend to believe that they themselves could never have the right, *therefore*, to try to stop these others from harming those persons, if they couldn't do that without having to hurt *them*. (They seem to worry that they might unjustly hurt innocent people...) But that would be forgetting one of the most important elements of the criterion, which states that one may do *anything* to others without being unjust — not only pleasant things, but also *hurtful* ones! — provided one is capable of behaving that way without any *contempt* — any *freely* chosen contempt towards the persons involved.

Another reason could also explain why people might find it difficult to recognize the validity of the "contempt-criterion", even though it is implied in their common conception of unjust acts, and that they often apply it themselves. That reason is a certain fear of the "relativism" that the frequently diverging *applications* of such a criterion would seem to confirm. How, indeed, could one understand the fact that many people are apparently able to subject themselves to (or to produce) an abortion, for example, or to "exploit" their poverty-stricken employees without any *contempt*, whereas just as many people are incapable of even *imagining* they could do such things, themselves, without having chosen to do them out of a personal contempt towards the persons involved? There are those, also, who are capable of treating people rather roughly, or of constantly imposing their will on them, but without their "victims" ever feeling themselves objects of contempt, while other people are sure that *they* could never act that way without having chosen to let themselves be *personally* contemptuous towards those persons.

A final example, perhaps more disturbing, should be familiar to most people. I was quite capable of lying to certain others yesterday, without the least bit of contempt towards them, whereas today, and without there being *any observable change* in the circumstances, I feel sure I couldn't possibly keep on lying to these people, unless I allowed myself to have a really personal contempt towards them. I may be surprised, but I must admit, upon reflection, that I still cannot see where my feeling could have gone wrong...

It is this apparently erratic behavior of the "contempt-criterion", its lofty independence of all circumstances, which makes it so suspicious to many. How could I understand that a behavior of mine which would be definitely unjust today, might very well *not* be unjust tomorrow? (Why, then, should I always *wait* for such a change?...) How is it possible to understand that an act which I would certainly consider unjust as coming from me, would *not* be judged unjust by many others, whereas *the opposite* might very well be the case in a couple of months, or a couple of decades? How can one avoid becoming a skeptic in matters of justice, when one realizes that many of the people who sincerely thought themselves capable, some years ago, of doing certain things without any contempt at all towards others, now observe (just as sincerely!) that they couldn't possibly do those very same things without any contempt towards certain persons? (Towards *women*, for instance?...)

It must be conceded that in itself, the contempt-criterion never indicates any concrete behavior, or any particular attitudes that *no one* could adopt, in any circumstances, without freely deciding to deny his or her own personal consideration to other persons. It should be noted, therefore, that even though it were possible to know that *most* people have never been able to do certain definite things without feeling (and being) unjust, that wouldn't mean that it couldn't happen, some day, that these people (or others) became in fact capable of doing *the same* definite things without being unjust, or without any contempt towards the persons concerned. (Even widespread "constants" can, and do change!)

In other words, it is this *capacity* (or incapacity) to act without contempt which changes in unpredictable ways, and *not* the criterion for unjust acts itself. This capacity may vary from one person to another, and (for the same person) from one period of time to another. It may vary even though the circumstances, or the concrete modes of behavior remained apparently the same. As for the criterion itself, one could observe that it remains perfectly constant and universal, even in the most changing circumstances, and for very different kinds of acts or behavior. It always states the very same thing basically, which will "encourage" a particular act, or "warn" against producing it, depending on one's present capacities or incapacities. And that basic statement is: *no one* ever has the right, in any situation, to do any thing whatever, when he or she is incapable, at *that* moment, of doing that particular thing without any personal contempt towards other persons. That, then, would be the one and only *universal* criterion for just or unjust acts, the one and only natural law of justice. And being strictly universal, it is, in that sense, "objective" and "absolute". Concrete acts can be variably just or unjust, but that fact is not entirely *arbitrary*.

3. JUSTICE AND THE "SUFFICIENT" REASONS

Mutual relations in our societies would no doubt be improved if all citizens could discover, and verify for themselves, that the fundamental law, principle, or criterion of "natural" justice, is the one which was uncovered in the preceding section, even though it is only *implicitly* contained, most of the time, in our common judgments regarding just or unjust acts. It was stated as follows: one has the *right* to do any particular thing — and would therefore not be *unjust* in doing it —, if one is capable of doing it without any freely chosen contempt towards other persons. Many discouraging and anti-social misunderstandings could certainly be avoided, if this law of "non-contempt" was universally perceived as the truly basic and practical principle of justice, as opposed to the "non-damage" criterion which says, rather improperly and not too helpfully: one has the right to do anything at all, provided only that one doesn't hurt, harm, or inconvenience anyone else without sufficient reason.

Harms and sufficient reasons

Those who are quite content with the "non-damage" principle of justice can point out the fact that people spontaneously consider as unjust, acts that are unnecessarily *harmful*. Some of them appreciate the fact that such acts — as opposed to personal intentions or attitudes — are often observable, and can therefore be the objects of confident judgments concerning the unjust acts of *other* people, as well as the objects of "corrective" penalties. But since it is commonly conceded that one can have a "sufficient" reason to cause *harms* to others, then it must also be conceded that "causing harms to others" cannot be, by itself, that which *makes* a person's acts unjust (or that which *is* unjust). It is indeed obvious that one cannot *define* unjust acts as "harmful acts that are produced without sufficient reasons", and then consider the sufficient reasons as that which enables us to produce harmful acts (and therefore "unjust" acts!) *without* doing anything unjust.

From a purely logical point of view — and also in accord with our common convictions about unjust acts —, it thus appears that one does nothing *unjust* when causing harms to others while having a sufficient reason to do so. But what is more importantly implied, here, is that harms, and acts which cause them, are never *themselves* just or unjust, and that the reason why they "become" just or unjust has therefore to be sought elsewhere. That reason could be, in general, that besides causing harms to others, one would also be doing something else, this "something else" being precisely what one wouldn't have the right to do (or would be unjust in doing). As for the "sufficient" reasons — when one actually has them —, they would turn out to be that which enables people to cause harms to others *without* doing the particular "something else" which they wouldn't have the *right* to do.

The most common "something else" that people also do when causing harms to other people, and which might perhaps be a sufficient reason to consider those harmful acts as not unjust, is that they thereby avoid causing *greater* harms to other people, or harms to *more* people; or they avoid bringing about even more harmful consequences for the future; or they promote, by these very harms, a greater "good" for society as a whole. But such facts — greater harms, and the greater "good" — are so difficult to evaluate and balance, that people — including specialists! — very often cannot but remain actually *unconvinced* about the results obtained, and even more so, in practice, about the "sufficiency" of the reasons that these results should be supporting. However, when people actually do become convinced during their search for really sufficient reasons, they could also notice each time — as will appear in the following pages — that it is because they had suddenly become convinced of being quite capable of doing the thing in question, in spite of its harmful consequences, *without* contempt for any persons.

An examination of our common experiences will now show that in situations of doubt, the capacity to act without contempt is the only criterion which can solve

— and does solve —, in a way which is totally convincing, the problem of the sufficiency or insufficiency of our reasons. The "something else" which one could be doing while causing harms to others, and which would make his or her harmful act unjust (even though the harms caused would sometimes appear *lesser* than they could have been), is the causing of these harms out of a freely chosen *contempt* towards the persons harmed.

The unpredictable sufficiency of the reasons

First, a few reminders and examples of the problems, doubts, and questions we sometimes have, and of the particular way they get solved. One of these examples will be illustrated in detail, thus allowing a closer examination of the typical situation. Secondly, a study of the factor which immediately *determines* the moral "sufficiency" of our reasons, that is, the unpredictable capacity (or incapacity) to act without contempt.

It is quite natural, of course, to think of unjust acts as being the ones which cause damages or harms to others. When do people actually become aware that they wouldn't have the *right* to do what they intended to do? Isn't it when they notice that others would suffer a certain harm as a consequence? It also happens that we feel morally obliged, on such occasions, to modify or abandon our own projects, in order precisely to avoid subjecting those others to the anticipated harms. Having no doubts, we don't try to find reasons for having the right to cause those harms. We don't even try to understand *why* we wouldn't have that right, at this moment, since we definitely *feel* that we don't. So everything is quite natural, and obvious. (We will perhaps decide to cause those harms anyway, but knowing very well that we will then be acting *unjustly*, with regard to the persons involved.)

But things are not always that clear. Very often, one cannot help hesitating, and searching for really "sufficient" reasons, that is, convincing ones. There is the situation, for instance, where doing what one intends to do would harm certain persons, whereas not doing it would harm *other* persons. Let us suppose I *don't* want to be unjust to anyone. What, then, should I do? On which side would the harms or damages be greater? Which *kind* of harm would be the worst? Which damages would have the most serious consequences in the future? The answers I find, one after the other, can't really convince me, and the reasons which might support them remain stubbornly insufficient. Having had time to consult others — even a few experts —, I had to face the fact that their answers or suggestions didn't agree with each other, and that none of them could help me to decide anything. Finally, all I could think was that the whole thing seemed totally arbitrary. (No, I am not at all scrupulous, nor particularly righteous: I would just like to *know* what I am doing!...)

To be personally reminded of similar situations, one has only to glance at the following cases:

- These rich people wouldn't even notice if I stole a few of their belongings, in order to help a couple of families in great need.

- I could save the lives of these three psychopaths, but to do so I would have to let die a very promising young cancer researcher.

- Being inclined to think that I have the right to keep the important sum of money I have just found, but not being sure enough, I wonder if I should seek the "impartial" opinion of a shrewd but honest person, or if — I'm in a hurry! — I should toss heads or tails. (Would these two solutions be so very *different*?)

- It would be "heroic" for me — but feasible enough — to abandon my career as a young social worker, so as to look after my severely handicapped sister who constantly begs me to do so.

- None of the reasons I could think of for having or not having the right to abstain from helping this person, have been able to strike me as being truly sufficient. And yet, I still feel that I *don't* have the right to refuse (even though I realize the *arbitrariness* of such a feeling).

If these problems don't just disappear (my handicapped sister unexpectedly died of a heart attack), there is a good chance that I will have the feeling, all of a sudden, of not having the right to do one of the things considered, and of having the right, therefore, to do at least one of the others. That feeling may have come up with the discovery of a new element in the situation, or of the sufficiency of a reason which until then seemed rather inadequate. But it may also have come up — as in the last case — without my having noticed anything *new* in the situation, or in the reasons already considered. At any rate, I cannot really understand *why* I got this feeling, since nothing seems to justify its occurrence. As a plain psychological fact, it remains arbitrary, while continuing to impose the irresistible conviction of *not* having the right to do one of the things considered.

Let us say that someone actually chose to act *against* this conviction. (Why not? Humans are free, aren't they?) One might want to ask what *reason* this person could have had, to make such a choice. But is it really necessary that one *had* a particular reason? After all, didn't the conviction itself occur without any reason? Isn't it purely *arbitrary*, just as the content of the feeling itself would seem to be? Wouldn't this person have the right, therefore, to act as he or she happened to prefer, or quite arbitrarily, and whether or not that contradicted the arbitrarily imposed feeling and conviction? Or should one think that this conviction, especially, has really *changed* something in the more global situation of the person?

In many cases, one could easily notice that this conviction actually *has* changed something. At least one thing: even though it is a purely psychological and arbitrary fact, it nevertheless happens to force the person to *take a stand*, by himself or herself *alone*, concerning other persons. The arbitrary feeling of not having the right to cause these harms to these particular persons, and the irresistible conviction which arbitrarily confirms it, can actually force the person itself to become aware of the fact that he or she would be quite incapable of harming these persons, at this moment, without having freely chosen to do it out of a truly personal *contempt* for them.

One could also note, at the same time, that it is this immediate incapacity — and *not* the harms themselves — which makes it impossible for a person to have the right to do what would harm other persons. Having noted this, one can then understand why it is that all reasons based on evaluations of relative harms (or the overall "good") — evaluations meant to confirm or deny a particular right — can turn out to be "sufficient" *or* "insufficient", without *that* fact having to be considered *arbitrary*. (Here again, everyone would have to verify or perceive all this by himself or by herself, especially the people who cannot remember having had similar experiences before...)

As could have been expected, a closer examination of the particular situations where we cannot avoid harming certain people *or else* certain others, and where we apparently have to balance the different harms (or to *imagine* what would generate the *greater* common good), has enabled us to discover the factor which actually *determines*, each time, the sufficiency or the insufficiency of any reasons we might have. That factor, as we have seen, is our current capacity, *or* incapacity, to act without any personal contempt towards others. And it also appears to be the only one, whether or not we happened to be well aware, each time, of its critical insertion, and "operation", in the very midst of our other various reasons.

No one would ever have the *right*, then, to do whatever would be necessarily accompanied by an attitude of contempt towards others, not even when this contempt would be "lesser" than the one which would have accompanied any other activity. The law of non-contempt just doesn't work that way: if someone chooses to do what would cause harms to some people, but only to avoid causing greater harms to others — that person being convinced that he or she couldn't cause these greater harms without being contemptuous (or unjust) towards those others —, then he or she would have *no contempt at all* (not even a "lesser" one) towards the persons to whom they were causing those *lesser* harms. In other words, the law of non-contempt doesn't require that we estimated and balanced the different "weights" or intensities of our contempt, in order to establish which activities would be accompanied by a lesser contempt and would therefore be "just" (or "less unjust"), since *no* contempt, towards *any* person, could ever be just. (That law is very different, of course, from the "utilitarian" principle of just or unjust policies, institutions, or activities, whose application to *concrete* situations requires an (impossible) evaluation and balancing of the harmful consequences.)

Many objections and doubts may arise at the thought of unjust acts being essentially — or "only" — acts of freely chosen *contempt*. For instance, one may fear that people would acquire much too easily the right to cause any kind of harm to others. It seems, indeed, that all they would have to do when they noticed that their acts would be harmful to others, is to carefully avoid having any contempt towards them. They could always say to themselves something like this: "If I do such and such a thing, it isn't because I want to harm these people, or because I have no concern for them. All I want, really, is simply to live my own life as best I can. If I could always do that without causing any harm to anyone, I would certainly be all the happier. In fact, I sincerely hope that everything I do will be the least painful for other people, or that they will soon be able to forget all they will have had to suffer because of me".

If we could always maintain a true concern for the others when causing them any kind of harm, or sincerely say things like the ones just quoted, then we would in fact have all the rights we could imagine. The trouble is, of course, that we often feel ourselves quite *incapable* of doing such and such a thing, right now, *without* having a really personal contempt towards other people. But what about this incapacity itself? To answer this question, let us now examine, as announced, a situation meant to illustrate, more in detail, what often happens when we try to determine whether or not we have the *right* to cause certain harms to others. The proposed investigation should bring out the fact that the right to do any of the things we could do without any contempt towards others is a strictly universal and immutable right, whereas our numerous other concrete rights are in fact subject to all sorts of *changes*, since they are determined by the obvious but unpredictable changes in every person's capacity (or incapacity) to act without contempt.

Since a few weeks, now, I've been wondering what I should do. I could certainly increase my turnover and personal benefits, if I decided to cut the salaries of my employees. But that, I know, would force them to live a much more difficult life. As for me, I really don't think I would be seriously inconvenienced if I chose to leave things as they are, at least for the moment. All the same, I still wonder if I wouldn't have the *right* to impose those hardships on my employees, or if, on the contrary, I would be *unjust* to them in cutting their salaries. (I do want to avoid being unjust, of course, at least "too" unjust...) What are the observations and thoughts that now come to my mind?

At first, these. Unemployment is still very much on the rise, and yet all my employees have a permanent job. Besides, the difficulties they would suffer couldn't be too serious, even though they would certainly be more serious for some of them. And if the circumstances got better, I could probably increase their salaries without too much of a delay, and even raise them to a higher level than the present one. Also, any increase in my business volume would be a contribution to the economic development of the region. So the more I think of it, the more I am persuaded that I actually have the *right* to go ahead with this programme.

After a few days, however, I start hesitating again. Some of the employees will definitely have a much more difficult life. True, they never trouble themselves with any family budget, they aren't too resourceful or clever, they can't get organized like many others. But is that a reason for me to let my business vegetate? If I really had to concern myself with all the neglectful or incompetent people, it wouldn't be long before I had to abandon any really interesting project... Would that be reasonable? And no, I really don't believe that what I've just been thinking is only an excuse. It could even be that my employees became more realistic once the salary cut were effective, and finally decided to get organized so as to eat better, yet less expensively, to clothe themselves and have fun just as well as before, but at a much lower cost! In any case, I should perhaps give more thought to the whole thing: maybe I *could* boost my business without cutting the salaries, and even without having to increase anyone's task. Of course, that would cost me a few more worries and more work, and that, I must say, is something I really don't find too attractive... But I'll still give the situation some more thought.

That is where I now stand. I was induced into comparing the various harms and inconveniences for my employees, my business, myself, or the region, with the hope of discerning my rights, or what justice itself would suggest or demand, in similar circumstances. The result is rather poor: only a certain number of maybe's! And I can't even say I went very far in anticipating and comparing the *future* harms, where the maybe's would obviously be more numerous and difficult to interpret... One may wonder, then, how this search, this deliberation, could ever *come to an end* — and otherwise than by the fact that I got carried away by some sudden and thoughtless impulse (whether or not accompanied by a guilty conscience), or that I had simply sold my business in order to take up some other project.

One could fairly anticipate that if nothing of the kind happens, there will come a moment — sooner or later — where I will certainly have to believe (and *will* believe) something definite enough about having, or not having, the right in question. And I will also decide to act according to, *or* against the indications of this particular belief. If I am still generally concerned about not being "too" unjust, I will sincerely believe, for example, that the situation being what it appears to be, I may "reasonably" think that I do have the right to lower the salaries of my employees. (In any case, I intend to see what can be done for those who would suffer the most.)

Certain considerations, certain evaluations — as "impartial" as possible —, will have helped me eliminate my latest doubts and objections. But I might then realize that a *longer* examination of the situation would perhaps give rise to new objections against my right, and possibly insurmountable ones. I might also notice that I really have no idea of the *exact* harms my employees would have to suffer. Even though I remained quite aware of this ignorance and of the risks it involves, it could still have happened that I discovered, somewhere along the line, reasons which appeared quite *sufficient*, at last, to guarantee that I actually had the right to lower the salaries.

A question may now come up, especially for persons who have already noticed that such doubts, questions, observations, and *changing* beliefs often do occur as just reported. That question is the following one: "What is it that happened, after a while — and in spite of my unanswered objections —, so that my dubious right could appear as *definitely* authentic?". I knew very well that I had not anticipated *all* the harms that would be suffered — especially the more distant ones —, but I also realized the impossibility of such a task. It therefore seemed fairly "reasonable" (or quite "sufficient") that I should stop at a certain moment, and in fact, at the moment I actually stopped.

But what happened at that particular moment? How could I have known, or even believed, at *that* moment, that I had traced a *sufficient* number of harmful consequences, that I had compared them *well enough,* and spent a *sufficient* amount of time at the task, to be assured that what appeared to be a genuine right of mine, at that moment, just had to *be* one, and quite definitely? Could I say that I had *seen* that the number of anticipated harms was sufficient? That their relative seriousness had been well enough evaluated? That the time I had spent, doing all that, had been reasonably sufficient? The answer, of course, has to be negative. (I *saw* nothing of the kind!) What actually happened is that I suddenly sensed, or felt, or understood, that I definitely had (or didn't have) the *right* to lower the salaries of my employees, and that all I had done up to now, in order to discover the answer, could "therefore" be considered as quite sufficient.

One might also add that what has just been related implies, in agreement with our various experiences, that our sudden discovery of the answer may occur after a long investigation *or* a short one, and independently of the fact that we had used appropriate *or* rather inappropriate means (whatever *that* could mean!). It even happens that we *cannot* succeed in finding a convincing answer... In any case, our initial question finally turns out to be the following one: "What is it that happened to me, and which could have made me suddenly *feel* or *understand* that I, let us say, *did not* have the right to lower those salaries?".

This is what could have happened in fact: I became gradually aware, and then all of a sudden very definitely aware, that if I decided to lower the salaries, that would certainly mean I would be *quite ready*, according to my present dispositions, to do so without worrying at all about the hardships that some of my employees would suffer, and in fact without even wanting to have a minimum amount of concern, or personal "consideration", for those employees *themselves* (or for their own *persons*). It is precisely this lack of consideration, this "contempt", which I more importantly felt as not having the right to make my own, nor to *express* by concretely harmful decisions or acts.

If someone were to ask me *why* I was now so sure I didn't have the right to lower the salaries, I would probably just say: "Because some of my employees would have to suffer, as a consequence, harms which would be *too* serious". But that would be a spontaneous answer, and one which did not mention *how* I suddenly (and finally) discovered, after having hesitated so long, that those harms were definitely "too" serious. Yet, if someone were to ask me whether the *principal* reason might not have been that I just couldn't imagine myself being able to cause those harms without any *contempt* towards my employees, I would no doubt have to acknowledge that that reason was in fact the truly basic one.

But suppose that a few days later, I had become convinced of *having* the right to lower the salaries. The main reason would have had to be the capacity I had suddenly acquired to cut those salaries, while actually maintaining a real concern for the future of my employees, or a true consideration for their persons themselves. Does that mean that if I had always been able to maintain a general concern for all my employees, I would have had the right, therefore, to do *anything* I wanted, as if none of the harms they would suffer could ever deprive me of any *right*? Basically yes; but in fact no — or not all the time. For it happens, more or less frequently, that people feel themselves incapable of doing such and such a thing, while *maintaining* their general concern and consideration towards all persons. Incapable, for example, of cutting the salaries of their employees, or of keeping them that low any longer, without having to *put an end* to the personal consideration they had for them. When that kind of incapacity affects them, they also lose the corresponding rights, and actually feel or understand that they do.

It also happens, at other times, that people feel themselves quite *capable* of doing the very same thing, or things even more harmful, while maintaining their consideration or concern for the persons involved. In cases where the harms seem more serious, it even happens that these people are able to *intensify* their concern for those persons, and to express it more concretely, for example, by improving the working conditions of their employees, or simply by engaging in sincere and friendly conversations with them. At any rate, the most important point to note is the *unpredictable* character of the capacity *or* incapacity that each one of us would have, at various moments, to do such and such a thing without any contempt towards other persons. One may try very hard to get rid of such an incapacity — for instance, by trying to think of universally accepted reasons, or of totally new ones, which would *sufficiently* prove or confirm the right that he or she might now have — but only to discover, very often, that none of the reasons which come to mind are really convincing...

What can happen, then, is that one becomes more than ever convinced of having this perhaps annoying, yet (presently) insurmountable incapacity. "But how could I have had the impression, up to now, of *having* that right? Would I perhaps make a mistake in believing I don't really have it any more? Have I perhaps become scrupulous, or too sentimental?" — The answer to the last two questions finally remains, very often, a definite *no*! "How is it, then, that other people (some of them quite perceptive and sincere) seem to know as a fact that *they* have that right? Would I be the victim of my education, of my present convictions, or is it that my psychological makeup contains too much subtlety, diffidence, or too great a bias?" — Again, the answer is often no; or that, *in any case*, I must be content with the conviction that *I* don't have the capacity to do this thing (at least this time) without having to abandon all *personal* consideration for other people. I may be surprised and more or less irritated by such a fact — and even end up by freely choosing to do what I felt I had no right to do —, but I cannot *deny* that I have the particular incapacity which I *feel sure* I have.

The subjectivity of the reasons

Many people are rather surprised, if not disappointed by the fact that there is no general agreement concerning the *rights* that each and every one of us would have, in the various circumstances (or in the more frequent ones). In fact, some people believe that *they* would have the right, like anybody else, to cause such and such a harm in the present circumstances, while others believe, on the contrary, that *they* wouldn't have that right, just as no one else either. (The disagreement is more obvious, for example, in the case of mercy-killing, capital punishment, life imprisonment, abortion, tax evasion, the promotion of capitalism or socialism.) Such disagreements could be explained in different ways, depending on whether or not one believes that there is a *necessary* bond — and therefore an *immutable* one — between the particular harms which people would have to suffer in the various kinds of circumstances, on the one hand, and the fact, on the other hand, that each of us would (or would not) have the right to cause the same harms, in similar circumstances.

Let us suppose that there actually is such a necessary and immutable bond. How could we explain the fact that people often *disagree* about many rights? Wouldn't we have to think that some of these people are wrong? Their mistake, or delusion, could be "explained" — provided we knew on which side it was! — by presuming that *these* people, for instance, are not perceptive or rational enough, or not sensitive enough (or else *too* sensitive?); or that they are in some way ill, or mentally deficient, or prejudiced, and so on. If they should persist in believing that they have to disagree, in spite of all the efforts of the others to make them realize their mistake, then these others would have to *conclude* that their belief is certainly *false*. Some of them will perhaps concede that those people might have a purely "subjective" right, but will have to maintain (because of that supposedly necessary bond) that it can *in no way* be a truly "objective" right.

As for the people who would not be making a "mistake", it seems that if such a *necessary* link existed, then one would have to grant them a rather odd capacity. Suppose, for instance, that some of them were quite sure that they had the "objective" right to cause a certain harm to others, and decided to do so. But while doing so, they also chose, of their own free will, to cause that harm as an expression, to their victims, of the personal contempt they had towards them. (And suppose they even took pleasure in acting that way...) Well, why not? Didn't they *know* that, come what may, they always had the "objective" right to cause that harm, because of the necessary and immutable bond there exists, each time, between our rights and the present circumstances? The same thing could also happen, of course, if one believed in the existence of such a bond between the observable circumstances and anyone's *capacity* (or *incapacity*) to cause harms to others *without* any contempt towards their persons. Here again, no disagreement should be possible. When one does arise, the only "explanation" would have to be that the capacities or incapacities of some people — always "the others"! — are somehow abnormal, or due to a current defect.

Now why should one believe, so obstinately, that the bond is necessary and immutable? Haven't we noticed before, in a number of *similar* situations, that we sometimes believed we actually had the right to do a certain thing which we then believed, at other times, we certainly *did not* have the right to do? We didn't know *why* such changes had occurred, yet it is a fact that we were often unable to *doubt* that we had the right in question. So why not stick to that *fact*, and recognize that, in spite of a certain number of observed constants (which are never strictly *universal*), the bond is simply *not* necessary and immutable? To be in accord with many of our experiences, we would then have to say that our rights (and our moral obligations) depend more exactly on our changing and unpredictable *capacity* (or incapacity) to act without any contempt towards others.

This "subjectivity" of our capacity or incapacity seems to contradict a widespread intuition: our rights should be *universal* (or "objective"), that is, the same for all human beings who are in the same circumstances, and therefore totally independent of each individual. But isn't it a fact that our individual capacities or incapacities, although not *publicly* observable, are also an actual part of the "circumstances"? So where would there be a contradiction, if we could say that *all* human beings have the right to do any particular thing — even a harmful one — whenever they are capable of doing that thing without any contempt towards persons? This would be a strictly *universal* law, since it would apply to all human beings without *any* exception (or whichever might be, for example, their personal abilities, qualities, or deficiencies, their social standing, or the laws and customs of their society).

Although universal, these natural rights are still subjective, insofar as they depend on each individual's capacity, at each moment, to act without contempt. If one means, by "objective" rights, the ones which would be independent of each individual's subjectivity, and the same for all human beings in all the same publicly observable circumstances, then of course none of our concrete rights could be considered as "objective". But if one means, by "objective" rights, the ones which would be independent of any person's *free* will and *free* choice, then all our various rights would have to be considered as "objective". For it obviously depends on none of us that we should be *capable or not*, at any moment, of doing such and such a thing *without* any personal contempt towards others. That capability (or incapability) is a fact which simply occurs, persists, or disappears, without our own free will ever having the possibility of doing anything about it. At any rate, this kind of "objectivity" happens to be precisely the one which we absolutely want to consider as an indispensable characteristic of all genuine rights — perhaps because of our conviction that no one should be allowed to *decide* what he or she, or the others, would or would not have the *right* to do.

There is no doubt something disturbing about the fact that some people would have the right to do what others would not have the right to do. How, indeed, could one actually approve the fact that some people often had the capacity to do certain things without any contempt, whereas others didn't have that same capacity? Shouldn't one think that this *unequal* distribution of capacities and incapacitites is in fact arbitrary, *unjustly* arbitrary, and therefore unacceptable or at least suspicious? How could one even avoid thinking that such an inequality must be apparent, and due to the fact that some people *deluded themselves* about their own capacities?

It is true, however, that people are not excessively surprised, or disturbed, by the fact that certain persons are much more capable that many others, in such and such a field of activity. People are not even surprised — at least not for a very long time — when the most capable persons see their capacities dwindle or vanish, whether for a short period of time, or forever. It seems that such things simply happen, and that there is no need to conclude, each time, that those persons were in some way ill or deluded. So why, then, should we be particularly disturbed by the thought that a person, without being at all ill or deluded, had the capacity to do a certain thing without being contemptuous towards others, while none of the other persons had that same capacity?

On the other hand, it is also true that the *feeling* of having certain rights is especially apt to inspire quite a bit of suspicion. How could one trust anyone's "feeling", or, in general, any simple feeling? Couldn't a person merely feel himself or herself *incapable*, let us say, of doing a particular thing without contempt, while actually *having* that capability? Yet, haven't we noticed before that to *feel* oneself quite incapable of doing such and such a thing, is often to *be* incapable, in fact, of doing it? Consider, for example, the number one tennis champion who, in the middle of important finals, feels herself unable, all of a sudden, to concentrate her attention, unable to win or to really *want* to win. So she quits... Or the man who has never doubted he could swim across this lake — he has done it many times —, and who suddenly feels himself totally incapable of doing it now. (He doesn't know at all what could have happened to him: he has slept well, nothing ails him, he has no problems at the moment, and yet he feels quite *sure* that he is not at all in the proper shape.) Or the well known and well appreciated public speaker who has always been sure of his power to arouse a crowd as he wished, but who feels totally (and strangely) *incapable* of really wanting to launch himself this evening.

Whether or not these people were laboring under a delusion, whether or not their paralyzing fears were well founded, or their present mood simply neurotic, shall we really think that these persons *were* "objectively" capable, at that moment, of doing what they had done so many times before, and that their "feeling" itself was therefore illusory, or somewhat deranged, when it made them falsely believe that they were truly *incapable*?

One would rather conclude, I suppose, that something — no matter what! — had made these people *become* incapable, at that moment, of performing as before. Or incapable of concentrating themselves, and of having the same thoughts and beliefs, and the same confidence as before. Perhaps they actually had a temporary sickness, or a faulty perception; but it could also be that there was nothing specially different about them, excepting, of course, this feeling of incapacity. It is *this* feeling which would have made them actually *lose* their capacity, as it is also a similar feeling — one of *having* the capacity — which, in spite of a certain number of deficiencies, would have made them *acquire*, in the past, the capacity of doing what they are now doing so well, and that the majority of other people are quite incapable of doing.

Persons who have suddenly become incapable of doing what they had often done before may no doubt be encouraged by others. One can indeed remind them of certain things, or help them to concentrate themselves, especially when there seems to be no reason to believe that they had become ill, or seriously unfit, or that there is no hope that they could *overcome* certain fears or paralyzing moods. But one cannot always succeed in helping them that way (even if one had always had a great success in doing just that, up to now!). For there are times when nothing can be done, and when the persons who keep on believing and "feeling" that they are incapable simply remain *in fact* incapable. What, then, would be the point in thinking that such persons are *objectively* capable of performing as before, but that it is only a psychological incapacity, a purely "subjective" one, which keeps them from doing what they would *still* have the "objective" capacity to do? (Should we say that this purely subjective incapacity is an *illusory* incapacity, or that it, too, can sometimes be an "objective" or a *real* incapacity?)

So why should it not be the same for our individual capacity or incapacity to cause harms to others without having any personal contempt towards them? Here again, to *feel* ourselves incapable would be, very often, to have become *in fact* incapable. Or to have become "objectively" incapable. Why not? The feeling of this moral capacity (or incapacity) could of course be the consequence of a purely "subjective" and nonmoral incapacity — yet a truly insurmountable one — to see the situation otherwise, or to overcome a particular fear, or to modify a certain impression. By various remarks, observations, and stimulating words, others may enable a person to see the situation differently, to vanquish a fear, to experience other impressions or beliefs, and eventually to experience a moral "feeling" which would be *contrary* to the one that he or she already had. This person could then have become capable, for example, of doing without any contempt, at least here and now, the things which he or she, only a few moments ago, felt totally incapable of doing *without* any contempt. Why wouldn't all that be possible — and actually happen —

without the persons having to be considered, each time, as having suffered from a particular illness or delusion? [4]

But what about the universality and the objectivity of our favorite rights? All our various concrete and particular rights — such as the right to free speech and opinion, to bodily movement and integrity, to a decent employment and education, for example — are practically dependent on the "subjective" and *changing* natural obligations of each of the others (although some of these concrete obligations may be considered as remaining more extensively and persistently constant than others). However,the universality of our *moral* rights (and obligations) is still preserved, since these rights, when moral, always concern a particular contempt towards persons, a contempt which *no* individual ever has the right, in *any* circumstances, to freely choose to make his or her own. And their "objectivity" is also preserved, since it never depends on anyone's own free will and free choice, that he or she *had* the feeling of being capable, or incapable, of doing such and such a thing without any contempt towards persons, and therefore had, or did not have, the "objective" *right* to do that thing.

To finally understand how our natural rights and obligations — or natural justice itself — are universal and objective (and in that sense *not* arbitrary), one had at first to find their universality and objectivity where they are *actually* located, instead of trying to see them, for all sorts of practical or personal reasons, where they are *not* located... Incidently, haven't we always known from experience, but not without ever having any doubts, that our various natural rights and obligations were not strictly universal, and that all of them comprise subjective components as well as objective ones? The present study will try to show that this intuition need not worry anyone more than necessary.

[4] Perhaps a more surprising yet frequent case would be the one where two persons each felt the *right* to fight against each other, even quite vigorously. That could be, for instance, when two men had to draw their own child out of a situation from which only *one* of the children could come out alive. In such tragic cases, each of the parents could even feel the moral *obligation* to try his best to save his child, and would thus be able to fight *without* any contempt towards the other. Because they understand the situation, they can understand each other, and even succeed in *showing* their mutual sympathy and consideration. (Why should we believe that such situations cannot exist, and that one of the parents, at least, *must* be mistaken or insincere?)

Reasons as a complement

For a person to discover whether he or she would have the right to do such and such a thing, it seems that all that is required is that they asked themselves whether or not they would be *capable* of doing the thing in question *without* any freely adopted contempt towards other persons. As can be observed, all other reasons for having or not having a right always turn out to be insufficient *by themselves alone*, since arbitrary, and therefore open to endless questions and discussions. Each of these other reasons being indeed the result of a necessarily partial and arbitrarily ended examination of the circumstances, one may realize that the discovery of more data, or the anticipation of further consequences, could always *reverse* the outcome of the previous investigation. Do we have to think, then, that the search for these other reasons is always completely useless or meaningless? — Not in the least, since we often do want to find such reasons, either for ourselves, or to serve them to others. Even if we have to concede that such reasons cannot *demonstrate*, by themselves *alone*, the existence of a particular right in the present circumstances, we can still have the conviction that they frequently provide a valuable and effective help. But what would be the proper role of these other reasons, or the kind of help they could provide?

One should notice, at first, that we only need those reasons for ourselves when we have doubts and are afraid of making a mistake. That means that we would want to avoid, if possible, being unjust to others (or having contempt towards them). If I happen to have doubts at a certain moment, it is probably because I *already* feel and believe, or even *know* that I have the right to do a certain thing (or that I *might* have that right), but that I am not entirely *sure*. (A greater attention should be granted to the fact that doubts often concern things we somehow already know, but through a knowledge which is not presently accompanied by all the *desired* certainty.) But how does it happen that I start having doubts all of a sudden, and cannot neglect them (as I was able to do on many other occasions)? These doubts may have come when I became especially sensitive to a particular element of the situation — when I suddenly realized, for example, that the damages I would be causing to others were *much more serious* than I had first imagined. My attention remains focused on these *damages*, and I am really *surprised* that I should have the right to cause them to others, or that it could even be *possible* that I should have such a right. I am not at all convinced of *not* having it (or of being quite incapable of causing those damages without any contempt towards the victims themselves), but I am nonetheless disturbed, or apprehensive, precisely *because* I still believe that I have this particular right. Yet the fact also remains that I have doubts — because of those probable reasons —, and that I would definitely need a greater certainty, one which would loosen this tension, disperse the nervousness which makes me hesitate, and even paralyzes me.

It is at this very moment that I could be more than ever inclined to turn towards the *other* particular components of the circumstances or situation, in the hope of discovering one of the so-called "sufficient" reasons. Not reasons which, by themselves alone, would be sufficient to convince me that I actually had the present right (or was capable of acting without contempt), but reasons which would be truly able to disperse or weaken my doubts, my astonishment, or my fears, and would thus allow me to think and to act with more confidence. For what happens, in fact, when I actually find the reasons I was looking for? The damages that I would cause now strike me as so serious and objectionable, that it seems to me quite unreasonable that I should have this right. (That fact explains my surprise and apprehension.) But having then noticed, for example, that any other behavior of mine would cause damages just as serious, but to a *greater* number of people, I was able to think it reasonable, after all, that I should have this right. (Or at least *more* reasonable.) And so did it appear to me as hardly reasonable any more — or not at all reasonable — that I could still have doubts, or let myself be *so strongly* impressed by the damages I would inevitably have to cause to certain people.

In all similar cases — and they are frequent! —, it remains a fact that none of the reasons suggested by the components of the observable or imaginable situation *itself* could demonstrate, by themselves alone, the existence or nonexistence of any particular right. Such reasons may at most serve as a confirmation. Their role (when they happen to produce a definite effect!) is to neutralize or to reduce the impact of other more or less conscious reasons, and thus weaken our doubts, and disperse our hesitations and apprehensions. (The fact that a *majority* of citizens is convinced of the validity of a certain right often plays such a role, but not every time we have doubts.) And so is our confidence (in having the dubious right) renewed and sufficiently *confirmed*.

There is also the case, of course, where the discovery of new reasons is suddenly accompanied by the conviction of *not* having the right we thought we had. That could mean that we had now become *incapable* of doing without contempt what we had been able to do, some time ago, without any contempt at all. (Again, why should we think we actually had that incapacity at that time also, but without having noticed it?) Yet the fact that this sudden feeling of incapacity was preceded or accompanied by the discovery of a certain observable component of the situation doesn't imply that this component *itself* — or together with the other components — would have been the "sufficient reason" for us to have that incapacity, or to have lost that right. However, it could very well have been the sufficient "reason" why we didn't have to put up with any doubts, since *because of it*, we were not particularly surprised, and even thought it quite reasonable (although perhaps annoying), that we should *not* have that right.[5]

For people who happen to be more thoughtful and critical, the fact that a person feels really capable of doing such and such a thing without contempt towards others is the *only* reason which could be *sufficient*, in fact, for them to think they had the right to do that thing. Many other reasons — greater harms otherwise, more people hurt — can also appear sufficient, but *only* when the persons happen to be convinced, at the same time, of having the capacity to act *without any contempt* towards others. So when I am quite sure of having a right which people think I *don't* have, why don't I just tell them the basic reason: I sincerely feel myself capable of doing that thing, at this moment, without any contempt towards anyone? (If it so happens, I could tell them that I even feel morally *obliged* to do the thing in question, that is, I feel I simply could not *refrain* from doing it — at this very moment at least — without having contempt for other persons.)

---

5 This particular course of events is very much similar to the one we can observe in our dealings with *language*. When we have doubts and revert to a text, a sentence, or to some part of a recent conversation, in the hope of finding *sufficient* reasons to think that their meaning is in fact the one we believed it was, it often happens that it is while thinking about one word *only*, or a particular passage, a single inflection or gesture, that we actually become convinced — because of *these* sufficient reasons — of having correctly understood the meaning of the *entire* piece of language. Even in physics, for example, current theories are considered verified, or confirmed — or they are at least preferred to others — because of so-called *sufficiently* convincing reasons which were suggested only by a *very small* portion of all the observed phenomena. (And these more convincing phenomena are not always the same for *each one* of the specialists.)

The same question might also arise when people who are in doubt ask me to help them discover whether or not *they* had such and such a right. Why shouldn't I just tell them to see for themselves whether or not they had the *capacity*, at this moment, to do the thing in question *without* having any contempt for other persons? Despite the fact that all other reasons could be endlessly objected to — and often are —, why, then, do we naturally prefer to point out some of these other reasons, instead of referring to the only basically sufficient one? (There are cases or moments where we do, of course, mention this capacity, or incapacity to act without any contempt towards other people.)

The preceding questions could be justified by the fact that many of the "sufficient" reasons which people serve to each other seem entirely arbitrary, if not childish. How should we judge, for instance, the "sufficiency" of the outcome of having tossed heads or tails, of having taken a vote, of having resorted to "impartial" or "objective" arbitrators or judges? How should we also appraise the inevitably premature results of what should have been the *endless* (and therefore impossible) "utilitarian" calculations? At any rate, it is an obvious fact that we do resort to such basically insufficient reasons, and even feel morally obliged, at times, to do just that. Although the link between such reasons and our capacity or incapacity to act without contempt is not a necessary or constant one, yet there does exist a psychologically meaningful link between the two. If that kind of reasons is often needed, it is because we are naturally inclined to associate the *harms* which a person causes to others, with a *negative* attitude of that person — often a form of contempt — towards these others. Indeed, we don't usually harm or inconvenience people we like or appreciate, and we often feel the tendency not to worry too much about causing harms or annoyances to people we don't like, or who don't seem to deserve our consideration anyway.

Because of that psychological fact, we naturally expect, from people who cause harms to others while denying that they do so out of contempt, that they gave us reasons (or at least *tried* to give us reasons) which could somehow convince us that they actually had, in spite of the appearances, a true consideration, concern, or respect, for their "victims", and therefore the *right* to cause those harms. Such reasons usually refer to otherwise greater or more numerous harms, or to later and more harmful consequences. If we finally accept them as "sufficient", it isn't because those arguments have demonstrated the fact that these people actually had the right they claimed to have — since reasons of that kind could always be challenged, or rejected as "insufficient" —, but rather because the reasons given had helped us to imagine how people *could* be sincerely convinced of having the capacity to cause such harms *without* having any contempt towards their "victims".

The role of sufficient reasons of that kind is only complementary, not fundamental, yet socially most important. Not only do such reasons help to disperse our doubts about our own rights and obligations, but they also serve to drive away the feeling of suspicion which the victims or the witnesses of our harmful acts often experience, when we say we have the *right* (or even the obligation) to act that way. But more important, socially, is the fact that we *search* for such reasons for ourselves, we *ask* others to give their reasons, and we *offer* our own reasons to people who don't even demand them. That fact is often — but not always! — a natural manifestation of the *concern* we have, or would like to have (and maintain) for other persons. Even if our reasons cannot totally convince the others that we do have the right we say we have, we still hope that they will notice that we are earnestly and sincerely trying to convince them, and that they will interpret these efforts of ours as meaning that we don't want to be *unjust,* or to have any *contempt* towards anyone, nor even to give the impression that we didn't care at all whether or not *they* thought we were contemptuous. In other words, the search for, and the actual presentation of these complementary reasons can certainly promote a *mutual consideration* between an ever larger number of people, just as the refusal to bother with that kind of reasons can be the expression of a freely chosen contempt for other persons, and thus weaken the fundamental bond of our society itself.

* * *

If the results of our study are essentially valid, then one would have to say that our natural rights and obligations, as also the reasons we consider "sufficient" for believing we have them, are nor *arbitrary*, since they always depend, in the end, on our current capacity or incapacity to act *without* any freely chosen contempt towards others. (Everyone would have to verify this for himself or herself.) But these capacities or incapacities of ours can change — and often do — from one individual or from one moment to another, and even when no significant change would seem to have occurred in the situation itself. Having no *necessary* link with the particular circumstances, they remain fundamentally unpredictable, and therefore seem to arise or disappear in ways that are totally *arbitrary*.

Such an arbitrariness can often be disturbing; it even happens that a sudden incapacity to act without contempt will place the least contemptuous person in a situation where he or she is forced to make the most painful of free choices. What is the use, then, of having rights which depend on a capacity (to act without contempt) always liable to disappear when most needed, or on "sufficient" reasons which can always lose their sufficiency at the "wrong" moment? More importantly, what could be the use of a natural justice which would seem much more concerned about "attitudes", or personal "intentions", than about appropriate living conditions for everyone?

Should we simply resign ourselves to the fact, then, that "Total Indifference" appears to be the name of the fate which "presides" over everyone's personal "destiny", and over the destiny of our society as a whole? But how could we reasonably do otherwise, when we observe what goes on, or when we think of what else could always happen? The least we can say is that natural justice doesn't manifest very clearly, by its erratic distribution of our various individual rights and obligations, a "logic of expansion" which would promote a happier life for *all* the members of our society. But we should try anyway to discover, at this point, whether there wouldn't be a *positive* link, after all, between justice and a happy life, instead of deciding *in advance* (out of impatience? out of compliance?) that what we have, here, is an unanswerable question. It would probably help, however, if we first clarified the concept of "a freely chosen contempt", and then found the answer to the question why natural justice seems to promote, above all, the avoidance of this particular kind of "contempt", rather than the well-being of each and every one of us. The next two sections ought to show that such a pattern need not be considered arbitrary, nor particularly threatening for anyone.

4. CONTEMPT AND LIBERTY

A critical examination of the *reasons* we consider sufficient for accusing someone of being unjust (or for exonerating a person from a similar accusation) has shown *what it is* that we implicitly require for anyone to be considered unjust. One must have acted freely, and out of contempt towards persons. Once explicitly stated, people might be astonished by the fact that it is this law of non-contempt — a law residing "inside" each person — which would determine, by itself *alone*, what is just or unjust at any moment. Indeed, wouldn't such a law be nothing but a totally arbitrary and purely subjective fact, a law which we could therefore peacefully yet firmly neglect, at least in many circumstances? (But isn't this astonishment itself a purely subjective and totally arbitrary fact, and therefore just as negligible a fact as that law itself?)

One might ask, on the other hand, whether rights and justice in general are the *only* values which could govern those of our acts which affect other persons. Is it inconceivable that one could have the right, and even the obligation to be openly contemptuous towards persons who, according to *other* values, would undoubtedly deserve such a contempt? Wouldn't it be a good thing, for instance, if our political rulers (and all individuals and groups who had the required power) intensified those of their activities which would benefit the more helpless citizens, but indirectly harm or annoy their exploiters, and did that out of a "corrective" *contempt* for the latter? If not, how could we possibly approve, or even understand a law of non-contempt which is so inflexible in demanding the *respect* of persons whose antisocial behavior should rather make them *deserve* the contempt of all the others?

This surprising demand of the law of non-contempt, and these questions probably result from the fact that a "freely chosen contempt" is something which still remains to be clarified and more exactly described. To begin with, it should be differentiated from the *feelings* of contempt, for others, which happen to be experienced in fact. But this clarification might itself give rise to a more urgent question, that of knowing whether or not we *have* the capacity to choose and to act *freely*. As it turns out, the answer to this question is precisely that which will provide the answer to the preceding questions, especially in helping us understand why the law of non-contempt exists, has to be inflexible, and is not as arbitrary as it sometimes appears to be.

A "personal" contempt

Observing certain people — or simply thinking of them — may give rise to a feeling of contempt towards them. That can happen quite naturally, for example, when one is shocked by the particularly cruel or abusive treatment these people inflict on others. It can also happen, of course, to persons who can't help feeling superior to most others, and who are therefore specially apt to feel contempt towards incompetent people, towards bashful or clumsy people, and towards all those who seem incapable of ever accomplishing anything important in their lives. One should note, however, that in both of these cases, the object of such a contempt is not so much the persons themselves, as their *behavior*, or their physical or psychological *defects*.

One of the characteristics of this *feeling* of contempt is that, like most of our feelings and desires, it comes and goes, it persists for a while or appears for a few moments only, it becomes overpowering or remains rather quiet, and does all that without our having had anything to do about it. Even when we try to "work on it", we often cannot succeed in getting rid of it; and when we do succeed, we would have to consider ourselves lucky, since we certainly had nothing to do about the *moment* it actually disappeared, and can't even be sure it won't come back tomorrow, perhaps this time for good. (How, indeed, could we be sure of *that*?)

In other words, when people *have* a feeling of contempt regarding the behavior (or the defects) of other people, that doesn't necessarily mean that *they* are contemptuous towards those persons — or towards anything else —, since it might very well be that they had nothing to do about *feeling* that contempt. The feeling just came, exactly as a feeling of uneasiness — about having that feeling of contempt — could have come with it, as well as the desire to get rid of it (or to have it stay). One can see, then, why people who simply happen to have such a feeling of contempt cannot be properly considered as being themselves contemptuous, at least not as they would have to be if they had taken the initiative in making themselves become contemptuous, that is, if they had *freely* chosen, out of themselves *alone*, to have a contempt of their own, a truly *personal* one. Even though one can have a feeling of contempt without having had anything to do about it, one couldn't possibly have a *personal* contempt, towards others, without having freely chosen to have one. And this personal contempt, of course, is precisely the kind of attitude which no one would ever have the *right* to have towards any person, in any circumstances.

In order to become personally contemptuous towards others, one doesn't *do* something, doesn't *produce* a particular thing — a contempt —, whether it be "inside" oneself, in the world, in the whole of existence, or anywhere else. When a person *freely* chooses to be contemptuous towards others, that person does not produce an "act" of contempt, nor even the "act" of *choosing* to be contemptuous. He, or she, does nothing at all. When one happens to feel (and therefore have) the *moral* obligation of having no contempt at all towards others, that obligation is more precisely the obligation to *avoid* being personally contemptuous towards these others, and so, in practice, the obligation to *freely* choose to make oneself have the *personal* consideration, towards these others, which one doesn't have at the moment. In other words, one then has the obligation not to *refrain* from freely choosing to have (or to try to have) a personal consideration for those persons, that is, not to remain personally inert, and lacking in personal consideration towards them.

It is only in *not* choosing to make oneself have a truly personal consideration towards others, that one can become personally contemptuous towards them, and not at all in freely *choosing* to remain lacking in consideration (or in freely *choosing* not to freely choose to have that consideration). To become personally contemptuous towards others, one need not freely *do*, nor freely *choose* to do anything at all. Indeed, when persons are aware of *not* choosing to have that consideration, they are even incapable of *freely* choosing or doing anything else whatever — like going to the movies, for example, or even working for the poor. (The reason for this incapacity should appear in the following subsection.)

There is no doubt a sense, of course, in saying that persons who are aware of *not* choosing to have a personal consideration for others, are "doing" something: they are freely "choosing" *not* to choose to make themselves have a personal consideration towards them; or to remain personally inert; or even to persist in doing so. But such a proposition could only mean this: while rightly believing that they had the *capacity* of freely choosing to have consideration for those others, they *did not* produce that choice. However, the fact that they actually believed that they *could have* chosen to have this consideration but *did not* do so, that fact can be considered as the equivalent, for them, of having chosen to make themselves have a personal contempt towards those others, and of having actually *made* themselves have such a contempt.

The study and discussion of our common experiences have already shown that when people feel the moral obligation to avoid any personal contempt towards others — and also feel, therefore, the obligation to have a minimum of personal consideration towards them —, they are then irresistibly coerced into freely choosing *either* to make themselves have (or to "give" to themselves) a personal consideration for these others, *or else* to do nothing, that is, to remain *personally* inert. If the people who are thus coerced actually do remain inert, this inactivity of their own person is, in its way, a true contempt, since the *only* reason they *could* have had to remain lacking in personal consideration towards others, is precisely to remain in such a state out of a personal *contempt* towards their persons themselves. (Indeed, if they felt *morally* obliged to have a personal attitude of consideration towards the persons involved, then they were also convinced of having the *capacity* to adopt such an attitude. All they had to do, in the circumstances, was to use that capacity...)

Many people, of course, would often want to ask the following question: "But *why* should we choose, *always* choose, to have consideration for such and such a person, even when we feel morally obliged to do so? After all, don't we have the capacity to *freely* choose as we prefer, even when morally obliged?". Perhaps the persons who would like to know the answer to that question are not at all free, at the moment, to want to know the real answer... But maybe they *are* free, capable of free *choices*, and yet would very much like to get rid of annoying preoccupations, or maybe simply to *understand*. One thing is sure: in many circumstances, the answer to the question whether we *are* free or not, is not that obvious. But that, in itself, shouldn't be a reason for us to abandon (or to keep on *postponing*) the search for the conditions of *possibility*, at least, of free choices and free acts for all persons.

Conditions for a free choice

To act freely, it isn't enough that one decided or intended to do such and such a thing: one must also freely *choose* to intend to do it. One must therefore be capable not only of intending, but also, at the same time, of *not* intending to do the thing in question. Even if this small boy's mother really intended to take the sharp knife away from him, we would no doubt concede that she didn't *freely* decide, or intend, to do that. As matter of act, she probably didn't even have *the time* to choose between intending, or not intending to do what she did, and never even *thought* of any other possibility (for example, that of watching over him, while teaching him to be careful with a dangerous knife). One may very well ask, however, if we ever do have the possibility of freely choosing anything, even at the end of a long deliberation.

One may certainly have serious doubts about that. Let us suppose that I believe I have the capacity, right now, to do this particular thing *or* that other one. I might ask myself, quite naturally, what I will *choose* to do. After a few moments, I suddenly choose to do the first one. Someone else having asked me why I chose to do the first one *rather than* the other, I simply replied it was because the one I chose happened to be precisely the one that I, myself, *preferred* to do. (Why not? Didn't I have a choice?)

It seems, then, that I naturally chose to do what I *most* wanted to do, *already* preferred to do, instead of choosing what I didn't particularly care to do. After a few moments of thought and hesitation, I had come to realize that I felt definitely more interested in doing that thing than in doing any other one. Perhaps I also felt that doing it would be preferable in a certain sense, or that, in any event, I had the obligation to choose to do that particular thing. Maybe I also became convinced, just before choosing, that it would be decidedly more rational, or sensible, to make that choice rather than any other, or that it would even be totally absurd to choose otherwise. In any case, those were in fact my reasons, and it seems to me that they should be good enough to make anyone understand why I, myself, chose the way I did. After all, those reasons were very simple and quite natural. (But the question is: have I chosen *freely*?)

It would have been at least a bit strange, of course, if I had freely chosen to do the very thing I *did not* want to do at the moment; or the one for which I had no interest at all; or the one which it would have been irrational to do, if not totally absurd. But if thoughts like these had crossed my mind just before I chose, could I have said, at that moment, that I was really *capable* of making such a "strange" choice, or if, on the contrary, I would have had to admit that I was in fact *incapable* of a preference so absurd, and that all there was left for me to do, in fact, was to choose what I most wanted, what interested me most, and which appeared to be the only reasonable and natural choice?

The following observations may perhaps confirm the belief (or the fear?) that we would all be totally "programmed", predetermined, and quite incapable in fact of choosing and acting freely. I may notice, for example, that *I*, myself, desire nothing, want nothing, and prefer nothing, so far as I am *personally* concerned. In fact, I could also observe that it only *happens* that I desire what I desire, that I want to do what I want to do, and that I prefer what I prefer. It even seems that I never choose to *start* desiring or wanting what I (happen to) desire and want.

More particularly, one could have reason to believe that we never even *prefer* anything, at least personally. As a matter of fact, every time I want to do or to obtain a certain thing, it is because I *already* want to do or to obtain *something else*. And I want to do or to obtain this other thing because I *already* desire the more or less pleasant satisfaction which I will feel when doing or obtaining this particular thing. If, let us say, I want to go to Paris, it is because I want to visit some friends. But I want that, because I already desire the feeling of enjoyment I know I will experience in meeting them, or in obtaining from them what I would like to obtain. (The reason could also be that I desire the satisfaction I know I will experience in helping those friends, or in having them enjoy the satisfaction that *they* will experience in receiving my help.)

In all these cases, there is no doubt a sense in saying that *I* didn't want or desire those feelings, at least not *personally*, since I didn't want or desire them out of my own *free* will. (The fact that it isn't this table, or my neighbor — but "*I*"" — who wanted and desired them cannot mean, of course, that I wanted or desired them out of *my own* free initiative...) When I first started to desire or to want those feelings, it wasn't because I had freely chosen to *make* myself desire or want them, nor because I had personally chosen that it would be *those* feelings (rather than others) which I would desire and want. It simply *happened* to me that I desired such feelings, so that strictly speaking I couldn't have said, afterwards, that those were *my* desires, the ones that *I* had freely and personally chosen and preferred to have.

Even though I hardly ever cease desiring and wanting all sorts of things, day after day, yet I seldom even think of asking myself whether I should choose to make myself desire and want any of them, or *not*. It seems that I have to conclude — or finally just realize? — that it is always *something else* (no matter what) which makes me start and continue desiring and wanting what I happen to desire and want. In other words, all my desires and preferences are actually *forced upon me*, quite irresistibly, and whether or not I happen to be aware of it. We are all puppets which happen either not to resent the fact, or to be predetermined, on the contrary, to be strongly irritated by the mere thought of such a possibility.

One may concede that we never choose to have or not to have our desires, yet still think that there are at least a few *preferences* which we could freely choose to make our own (and even succeed in doing so). Consider someone, for instance, who has had a particular desire for many years, and has been able, most of the time, to satisfy it quite enjoyably. Since a few months, however, that same person doesn't seem capable of satisfying it any more — or perhaps manages to do so every now and then, but without feeling any real enjoyment. So he, or she, starts trying to satisfy some other desire instead, or to get interested in something new and more pleasant. After having thought about that for a couple of weeks, and compared the more promising possibilities, that person finally *chooses* to get interested in a particular activity, succeeds in getting actually interested in it, decides to *prefer* it to any other possibility already examined, and is even capable of producing it quite often. As a result, that person prefers the selected activity more than any other, and actually enjoys it much more than he, or she, could presently enjoy anything else.

Has this person *freely* chosen to get interested in that activity, and to prefer it to all others? Has this person freely chosen even to *try* to acquire another desire, a new interest, a new preference? If so, *why* did this person choose each one of these things? Wasn't it because he or she could not help thinking, at a certain moment, that these things would probably *best serve* a certain purpose, which was the satisfaction of a desire that he or she *already had*? And wasn't this the desire to live a more enjoyable life, at least compared to the one which had become definitely less interesting, and even painful? The important point, here, is that this person already had a desire which was *more preoccupying* than any other (at least during that period), and whose satisfaction he, or she, could not help *preferring* to the satisfaction of any other desire. (Perhaps that person never even *thought* of choosing, or preferring, the satisfaction of *other* desires.)

The preceding observations have brought out this fact: whenever we choose anything — to go for a walk, eat something now, do something obviously irrational but exciting, start a new life, and so on —, we are *irresistibly determined*, by our latest desires and aversions, to choose and prefer what we (happen to) choose and prefer. One might think that if we had no desires or aversions at all, we could then *freely* choose to do anything we had the capacity to do. But that would be impossible, since having no interest in any particular thing or activity, we couldn't know *why* we would choose a certain thing rather than any other. (We wouldn't even be interested in choosing at random to do a certain thing "only to see what would happen", or "just for fun of it", since according to the assumption, we would have no desires or aversions, and therefore no interest in anything — not even in having fun, or in seeing what would happen. If we nevertheless did choose a particular thing, that could only mean that something else (than our desires, or than ourselves) actually *made us* produce that choice, whether we were aware of it or not).

The conclusion would be the same if we had many desires and aversions, but were never *irresistibly coerced*, by any of them, into choosing or preferring any definite thing. Of course, if our desires and aversions only *inclined* us — without forcing us — to choose or prefer a certain thing, one might believe that we would then have the capacity to choose, quite freely, *either* what we desired the most, *or* what we least desired (that is, repulsive things, or things we considered irrational or absurd). But that is impossible, since we would then be in the same situation as the one we have already examined, where we had no desires or aversions at all. Indeed, we would never know *why* we would choose the things we most desired, *instead* of the ones we desired less, or even found repelling (and vice versa). If the reason was that it seemed more rational or reasonable to choose what we desired *instead* of what we found repelling, that could only mean that we *could not* have chosen, at that moment, something we thought irrational, unreasonable, or simply crazy.

If some people still maintained that they could have freely chosen the irrational or the crazy, but freely chose and preferred the rational instead, that would have to mean that they had *made themselves* choose and prefer the rational, even though they could *just as well* have made themselves choose and prefer the irrational. But then *why* did they make themselves actually prefer the rational? And if they had made themselves choose and prefer the irrational, *why* would they have made themselves choose and prefer *that*? If they finally say that it is because that is what they wanted at the moment, then *why* did they make themselves choose and prefer what they wanted, instead of what they *did not* want (or vice versa)?

To maintain that a free choice is precisely what these people have made, and that they needed no particular reason to choose one way rather than any other (they are free, aren't they?), is simply begging the question. Choosing or preferring one way instead of any other *without a reason*, that can only consist in remaining fundamentally *indifferent* to whatever one would choose and prefer, and in being therefore swept away by whatever could tip the scales and thus *make one* "choose" and "prefer" what one doesn't *oneself* freely choose and prefer. (The "scale tippers" are no doubt, at each moment, our stronger desires and inclinations.)

It would seem, at this point, that to be able to freely *choose* a certain thing *rather* than any other, one must already have a reason, that is, a *preference*. But if this previous preference is always irresistibly forced on us, then we can "choose" and "prefer" many things, but never *freely*. The condition of possibility of any free choice would therefore have to be this one: we must be irresistibly *coerced* into freely choosing to *make* ourselves have a certain preference, *or else not* to make ourselves have that same preference. If we freely choose to have and to maintain that preference, we become capable of freely choosing and preferring many *other* things also; but if we freely choose *not* to have that preference, then everything we choose, prefer, and do *afterwards* could only be the agitations of pure puppets, of sophisticated robots. As one may suspect,the preference in question would not be the preference of anything whatever, but only that of "things" which *could* be freely chosen and preferred. But *are* there such things?

How, then, could we be irresistibly coerced into *freely* choosing to prefer something? There would be a contradiction, here, if we were irresistibly forced to freely choose to have a certain preference *instead* of freely choosing *not* to have it (or vice versa). But there would be no contradiction, of course, if what was meant is that we would be irresistibly forced to freely choose *between* making ourselves have, or else *not* making ourselves have a certain preference. Now for this kind of coercion to occur, it seems we would have to find ourselves in a situation where whatever we then did *or* did not do, we would inevitably have *freely* choosen and preferred, out of our own selves *alone*, to do it or not to do it. But what is it that has to happen, for us to become so coerced, and therefore capable of such a truly *personal* choice and preference?

An answer to that question is already contained in our own experience, particularly in the perceptions which often accompany our moral *obligations* of justice. It can appear more clearly in those of our obligations which concern people who are here and now present, and who could therefore interpret our behavior and attitudes as being just, or unjust.

Earlier in this study, we have observed that our *moral* obligations of justice, while obliging us to do or not to do certain things, happen to oblige us *more importantly* to have a minimum of consideration — or to have no contempt at all — towards the persons themselves. A moral obligation was then described as the sudden and unavoidable conviction, or feeling, that it is presently expected of us, as it were, that we gave ourselves a truly personal consideration for other persons *themselves*, that is, independently of the qualities or capacities they might have. The same description also included the conviction that the *only* reason we could possibly have for not giving ourselves this consideration, would be that we freely chose to *prefer* having contempt (instead of consideration) towards these persons themselves. This twofold conviction can become more vivid when the obligation we feel happens to concern people we actually see, people who are claiming something as a *right*, and who really *expect*, from *us*, not only that we did this thing, but that we did it, above all, out of respect and consideration for *them* (instead of doing it without "giving a damn" about *them*, about their own *persons*). In such cases, the obvious expectation of other people concerning our own personal attitude towards them can convince us, more than ever, of being really capable of *freely* choosing either to give ourselves the consideration they expect, or to refuse to do so. And that conviction also concerns the fact that we just *cannot avoid* making a choice of *our own*, right now, and having a truly personal preference.

In coercing us into freely choosing to have, or otherwise *not* to have a personal consideration towards others, moral obligations thus happen to coerce us into giving ourselves a freely chosen *preference*. (Moral values also do the same thing.)[6] Here, then, is a condition of possibility for free choices. What *must* happen, is that we became subjected to a moral obligation or value. As a matter of fact, that condition is even *the* condition of possibility for all free choices, or for liberty in general, since any other such condition would have to be an *equivalent* of this one, that is, a condition which could coerce us into giving ourselves a *freely* chosen preference. One should also notice, of course, that once people chose to prefer having a personal consideration for other persons (instead of a personal

---

[6] The main purpose of the following definitions is to differentiate a few of our common human experiences. We feel a moral *obligation*, when it is expected of us, as it were, that we *freely* chose to fulfill it. This expectation is a strict requirement, in the sense that one is then convinced that it would be wrong (or unjust) — but quite feasible — to freely choose otherwise. We experience a moral *value*, when it is likewise expected of us, as it were, that we freely chose to *make it* our own. But the expectation, in this case, is *not* a strict requirement, in the sense that one would do nothing wrong — only something not as good — when freely choosing *not* to act as expected.

On the other hand, obligations are purely psychological (not moral), when we are irresistibly forced to want (or not to want) to fulfill them — as when we are obliged to want to satisfy the *irresistible* urge to leave a room, to hit someone, or to adopt such and such a behavior. Values are also purely psychological, when we are irresistibly forced to make them our own, that is, when they are the objects of irresistible needs or desires. Finally, moral *rights* are the ones that others have the *moral* obligation to respect.

contempt), they could then freely choose to do (and could freely *do*) all sorts of other things, such as working for the poor, reading a book, drinking beer, and so on. So long as that freely chosen preference is maintained, one may indeed do these other things quite freely, provided only that there existed a consistent or rational link between doing them, and freely maintaining that original preference. (The link is usually "instrumental" : I choose to do this, *because* it should help me to maintain, extend, or enliven my own consideration for others, or *because* I want to inform them about this attitude of mine.)

Isn't it still rather strange, and even arbitrary, that the condition of possibility for choosing freely should concern a particular *attitude* of ours, and an attitude towards *persons*? Couldn't it have been something else, instead of this "consideration for persons" ? Why is it that it is only when "facing" persons, or at least having them in mind, that we could become coerced into choosing freely? We may note, to start with, that humans seem to be the only type of beings which *could* know or suspect, out of their own experience and need, what it is, for their person itself, to be the object of the personal consideration of others, and could therefore also know or suspect what it is, or what it could be to have consideration for the *persons* of the others (not only for their qualities or capacities). Even when the desires of human beings are often enough satisfied over a long period of time, it indeed happens to many of them to feel a certain *need*, one which is very different, in fact, from the need to become the object of the admiration, the respect, or the fondness of other people (or of the "affection" of their own cats, dogs, or horses). It is the need for their own *persons* to become, independently of their attractive qualities, their admirable capacities (or of anything else), the object of the respect, or of the truly *personal* consideration of other human beings.

Such a need is probably felt more or less frequently by most people, although many of them wouldn't be able to identify its precise object. However, as we have already observed, people could become more easily aware of it when they claim something as a *right*, since the bitterness and the indignation they experience and manifest on such occasions seem to indicate that they are anxious to obtain just that: the truly *personal* respect and consideration of the others, regarding their own persons. Having this need enables people to be more sensitive to persons in general, and also to the fact that every human being *could* very well need, at any moment, the personal consideration of others towards his or her own person. So much so, indeed, that when they, themselves, feel a moral obligation concerning such and such a person, they instinctively know, or at least suspect, that it is precisely *their own* free choice and *their own* personal preference, which is now expected and even "summoned", and that they couldn't possibly avoid deciding, out of their own selves *alone*, what they will *themselves* do. In fact, they are irresistibly coerced, at that moment, into freely choosing and deciding what their personal *preference* will be.

The fact that the condition of possibility for freely chosen preferences has to concern *attitudes*, and attitudes towards *persons*, thus turns out to be a fact which is not arbitrary after all. We have already noted that people who have no freely chosen preference cannot freely choose to do anything at all. That also means, of course, that they cannot even freely choose to give themselves a personal *preference* In order to *become* capable of freely choosing or doing anything, they would therefore have to be *coerced* into freely choosing *between* having a certain personal preference, and *not* having that preference. But to be so coerced, people would necessarily have to know what the point (or the difference) would be *in each case*. (If a person did not *know* that, then he or she would not know *what* to choose, and couldn't possibly *choose*.)

Now if it were a fact that human beings naturally feel, at times, the need for their own persons to become the objects of the freely chosen *consideration* of other persons, and if some of them suddenly felt morally obliged to give themselves such a personal consideration for some of the others (while naturally suspecting that these others might be needing it and hoping for it), then the ones who felt that obligation would actually be coerced into freely choosing *either* to give themselves the consideration in question, *or else not* to do so. They would now have become quite capable of such a choice, since they would *know* what the point of their freely chosen preference would be in each case: it would (or might) fulfill the need and the hope of these others to become the objects of a truly personal consideration; or, it would (or might) otherwise frustrate that same need and hope. The people so coerced could therefore freely choose and decide what kind of persons they will be: persons who prefer, out of their own selves, to have consideration (or a "positive" attitude) towards other persons, or else persons who rather prefer "not to give a damn" about them, or about persons in general.

It so happens that being coerced into freely choosing between *these* particular preferences is the *only* possibility, and cannot therefore be considered as an *arbitrary* fact. One could hardly imagine, indeed, how one could be coerced into *freely* choosing, and therefore *personally* choosing to get interested, let us say, in peanut butter rather than marmalade, in reading a book rather than playing tennis, or in things which — including plants and even animals — cannot *expect* (or hope for) our *freely* chosen and *personal* consideration towards them. Such a coercion (into freely choosing between preferences of that kind) is impossible, since one wouldn't have the slightest idea of what the point would be in choosing to have any of these preferences rather than any other, and therefore wouldn't know *which one* to choose.

It also happens that in coercing us into making ourselves have a freely and personally chosen preference, moral obligations of justice don't *limit* our liberty. The preceding observations and arguments imply, on the contrary, that they actually provide us — as moral values also do — with the *capacity* to choose and to act freely (out of our own selves *alone*), and therefore to live a life which we, ourselves, freely chose to live. (The following sections of our study will bring out the fact that any particular kind of *freely* chosen life can only be a *social* one, or one which, by its very existence, cannot but promote a *mutual* respect and consideration between *all* persons.)

Of course, moral obligations of justice often oblige us to limit, or even to give up entirely the satisfaction of some of the desires we happen to have. Although such restrictions can sometimes be painful or annoying, yet they cannot limit the *liberty* itself of our own persons. But couldn't it happen that, in wanting to fulfill all our moral obligations and values, we had to limit or give up the true satisfaction of the most important desire we had, and which is no doubt the desire to live a happy life? Is the constant fulfillment of our moral obligations of justice, and of our moral values *always* compatible with a sufficiently happy life? Some experts seem to think that the answer must be no, whereas other experts believe the opposite. So what shall *we* think?...

Experts, of course, are very useful people, and often indispensable ones. But is that true in any domain, or in any circumstances? When moral problems are concerned, can experts really give any definite solution, or only mention possibly relevant points which might help others better notice and understand *their own* present experiences, including their troublesome fears and their deeper aspirations? As will appear in the following section, these common fears and aspirations could only be dealt with, in the end, by the free and meaningful choice of each person itself.

5. JUSTICE AND THE HAPPY LIFE

Why is it that people who have a natural concern for other persons often hesitate to help them, and sometimes even do things which might indirectly hurt them? There are all sorts of reasons, of course, but let us consider the following one, very frequent and typical. Many people are often engaged in trying to realize a personal plan of life, having the conviction, in fact, that the constant pursuit and realization of this plan would be the surest way — if not the only way! — to live a truly happy life. They had thought of other plans of life, had even pursued some of them for a while, but had become ever more convinced that their present one was more realistic, less exerting or less often boring, and the one whose pursuit would enable them to live as happy as *possible*.

When the prospect of living happily for the rest of our lives is what is at stake, one can understand how anything which could seriously threaten it would be naturally *feared*, especially by people who are lucid and practical. Such persons would even tend to think that when happiness is concerned, all threats are too serious, and no *risk* should ever be taken. (Why should one suspect these persons of being abnormally fearful and even neurotic, or particularly egotistical? Besides, how do we know their plans of life don't actually include the happiness of many other persons, perhaps that of *all* other persons?...) It shouldn't be surprising, then, that because of this fear of losing their chances for a decently happy life, people sometimes decide (perhaps with a certain sadness) *not* to fulfill a moral obligation, or *not* to give up or postpone activities which would cause harms, or inconveniences, to other people.

One may suspect, however, that no particular activity, or plan of life, would be indispensable for a truly happy life. Hasn't it happened before, as a matter of fact, that persons had thought that they would be definitely unhappy if they had to be content with a particular situation, or with a certain type of activity, but only to discover that once "condemned" precisely to a similar situation and to that same type of activity, they actually experienced a joy and happiness as extraordinary as unexpected? It thus seems that people could live just as happy as each other, while pursuing activities that are quite *different*. But if that is so, what does a happy life exactly depend on, in each case? If we knew the answer to that question, maybe no one would ever "have to" cause harms to others, since we would perhaps have understood, at the same time, how a truly happy life for any one of us could be compatible with the possibility of a truly happy life for each and every one of the others. (Wouldn't our political leaders themselves have to *know* that, if they were ever to stop using lies, or inconsistent language?)

Desires and happiness

A happy life always depends, in fact, on whatever people happen to desire the most. Certain people desire above all to feel marvelously at ease in their own body and mind. They become miserable and worried when they feel the slightest pain, or sadness. Other people constantly yearn for something exciting or special to happen to them, something which would really enthrall them and make them soar. Unless that happens — and often enough —, they feel depressed, or absolutely wretched. Others couldn't be at all content with sensations of that kind (even "profound" ones), unless they were a consequence of their having accomplished important or "noble" things, or things they could certainly be proud of having accomplished. Other people are most happy, on the contrary, when they are living a quiet and peaceful life, in blissful harmony with nature itself, or with their fellow human beings, or simply with their own selves. (Vivid emotions make them nervous, painfully disturb them, and rapidly wear them out.) Finally, other people can only be happy when they know they are unconditionally loved and cherished, or when they, themselves, feel passionately in love, or when both of these happen at the same time. No other experience would be capable of satisfying them in the least, but could only appear to them as too superficial, much too colorless, and hopelessly boring.

The same person may of course feel *all* of these imperative desires one after the other — some of them making several reappearances —, yet without anyone being able to know in advance which ones will arise and disappear, nor which ones will predominate for a longer period of time.

Despite the differences between the particular happy lives that have just been described, one may nevertheless notice that they have two characteristics in common. First, this one: living the happiest life consists in living the life which one *most* wants to live. It does seem, in fact, that each and every one of us is living as happy as possible when he or she is doing, or obtaining, or feeling, what he or she, at any moment, most wants to do, to obtain, or to feel. But there is a second condition: people must never have the fear — the *serious* fear — of becoming unable to live, *for the rest of their lives*, the kind of life which, at the same time, they couldn't help wanting above all to live.

Incidentally, a prerequisite should also be added to these two conditions, that is to say, the indispensable presence of *desires*. If one never desired anything, if one were totally indifferent to anything at all, then one could never really want, nor will, anything in particular, and couldn't therefore live a *happy* life. Of course, one couldn't live an unhappy life either. (To think that life would be unbearably dull — and therefore miserable — if one never wanted anything (or were always indifferent to everything), is to be blind to the fact that one *couldn't* find life so dull, if one hadn't at least the desire to live the opposite of a dull life...) In any case, it is a fact that a great number of people have suffered from not having obtained, after many long years, the satisfaction of desires which they couldn't help wanting to fulfill. Some of these people have even tried, as a last resort, to make these desires *disappear;* not so much in the hope of becoming happy at last, but in the hope of at least not remaining unhappy for the rest of their lives.

No happy life, no fear, and no unhappy life would then be possible unless one had certain desires. However, one never chooses to have the desires one has: they arise or vanish, they become more intense or hardly felt, they succeed each other for long or for brief periods of time, without our having anything to do about it. One never even chooses to have the *thought* of taking such and such means to intensify them or to get rid of them. On the contrary, that thought *itself* — as any other thought or desire — always arises without our having anything to do about it. Nor does it depend on one's own self, that the means one happens to have thought of using (to intensify or to fulfill such and such a desire), are actually followed by *success*. Sometimes they are, and sometimes they are not.

Finally, one never chooses to want or to will what one *happens* to want or to will. Nor to want it for a long time, or for a few moments only. But if one cannot choose to *have* the particular desires one has, wouldn't it be possible for one to choose to *will* different things, like to do or to obtain such and such a thing, in order to satisfy a particular desire? One should notice, however, that the words "to will" simply mean, here, that one wants *more intensely* to do a certain thing, or that one is far more *determined* on doing that thing than on doing any other. And so it is that, whenever one is intensely resolved on doing a particular thing (rather than any other), the reason must be that one has a *desire*, and one which has become so overpowering and demanding — or whose non satisfaction is so difficult to bear —, that one cannot but absolutely *want* to fulfill it, or be totally *determined* on willing everything that would be needed for its actual fulfillment.

Having lived through difficult and even painful times, or having seen others plough through similar hardships, certain people have come to think, quite naturally, that they might perhaps be inhabited by a particular desire they have not yet noticed (because of the "clamor" of their other desires?), and which could be the one they would have to fulfill in order to live, at last, a happier life. Incidentally, why couldn't there exist, in fact, a desire more fundamental than any of the others, that is, more vitally constitutive of the sort of beings we are, and whose realization would enable us to live at least "basically" happy, or despite the fact, therefore, that our other desires often remained more or less partially and even painfully unsatisfied? The fulfillment of such a desire would not enable us to live perfectly happy, of course, although quite reasonably and *really* happy. At any rate, those persons are convinced that the subject is certainly worth looking into. (And so much the better, in a sense, if *other* people are happy enough, and often enough, not to feel the need to give it any thought...)

It would seem, then, that at least one thing is sure: it is *in fact* possible to live a "fundamentally" happy life, even when some of our other desires are not satisfied. That happens, for example, when people are in the way of realizing (without actually fearing any possible failure) the desire or the plan of life which they are *most* determined to realize. In such cases, it is of little importance to them that they have lost a leg, their job, or their elections; that others are scornful towards them, or that very few people take an interest in them; that is, *if*, in spite of that, they are in the way of completing the novel they are writing; or *if* this marvelous woman, or this extraordinary man, is responding to their hopeful advances with an ever-increasing affection or passion; or *if* they have obtained the assurance of continual grants for the social organization they preside. The happy life of these people is not *seriously* affected by the discomforts, the insults, or the vexations they have to suffer in such respects, since they are in possession of the essential: they are doing what they most want to do, without really fearing the occurrence of insurmountable obstacles. They are perhaps deluding themselves in having no fear of any permanent failure — they probably never even thought of such a possibility —, but the fact that they feel assured of "the essential" enables them to say *quite sincerely*, about the hardships they suffer: "Well so what? That doesn't *really* bother me!".

However, people who are living happily must not start realizing, all of a sudden, that their happiness is a haphazard thing, that they have been lucky — as compared with many others —, and that their luck might very well *change*, no matter what precautions they could have taken. As a result, their happiness could be indeed perturbed, not only by a deep fear concerning their own future, but also by the discovery of the fact that their happiness is a mere succession of the moods, and of the states of mind, to which they happen to be *subjected*. The mechanism of their desires and wants is followed by another mechanism: that of an interchange of sensations that are sometimes pleasant or even utterly gratifying, but sometimes painful or even excruciating. If they also happened to notice that they are, in fact, the playthings of an indifferent hazard — and will be for the rest of their lives —, and were unable to forget such a thought (such a possibility!), then a distressing feeling of personal *insignificance* could easily get hold of them — until a more familiar desire succeeded in diverting their attention, at least for the time being.

These people can actually *suffer* from the thought of being the playthings of an indifferent hazard? The prospect of their own "insignificance" would be that hard to take? Could it be that this suffering — or sometimes this simple but profound uneasiness — were the result of a more recently felt desire, one whose satisfaction would still have to come? But what sort of desire would that be? A more "fundamental" one? In other words, one which would be an indispensable part of what human beings happen to be? If so, then what kind of life would happily satisfy this particular desire?

A "fundamentally" happy life

Let us consider again the fact that people could be just as happy as each other, while living lives that are quite different. Each one of them — the actress, the social worker, the politician, the likable beggar — only has to be living the life that he, or she, would *most* want to live. The actress may be astonished by the fact that the politician really seems happy to live that sort of life, but that is because she simply couldn't imagine how *she* could want to live that way. (As for the beggar, he would probably be more amused, than surprised, by the fact that all those people had to work so hard in order to live a (dubiously) happy life...) Of course, not all beggars, I suppose, and certainly not all professionals, are happy. To be able to live happily, then, it shouldn't be necessary to have a special desire, nor that it should be this or that particular one. Indeed, it would suffice that one *happened* to feel a certain desire — no matter which —, actually wanted to fulfill that desire, and were confidently determined to obtain *its* satisfaction.

As already noted, however, it would be quite necessary, in order to live a "fundamentally" happy life — a life which would be as happy as possible —, that one were actually *determined* to obtain the satisfaction of a certain desire (more than that of any other). We now revert to that particular point. It happens to many people, indeed, that even for rather long periods of time, their habitual desires and willful efforts are continually realized, but that they nevertheless remain profoundly unsatisfied, and silently (yet truly) unhappy. They undoubtedly experience pleasant feelings and sentiments, sometimes even enthusiasm, yet without being able to see, in the concrete flow of their otherwise happy life, anything but a spectacle far more disappointing and boring, in fact, than delightful and marvelous. These people often reach the point where they can't even really *want* any of that any more; or if they still happen to want some of those things, they could atually say that *they,* themselves, don't really (or personally) care, and that, in a sense, *they*, themselves, are not at all *determined* on living that kind of "happy" life.

Groups of laboriously growing adolescents are by no means the only human beings who experience such a strange perplexity; many adults who are otherwise quite mature, and in a perfectly well-balanced emotional state, also do. (If we can't help seeing them as people who are definitely ill, we could perhaps try to find out what it is, exactly, that made them have *that* kind of "illness".) Although these people have noticed that they couldn't really get themselves determined on obtaining the satisfaction of any of their familiar desires, it is nonetheless obvious that they do have a particular desire, one which they would want above all to satisfy, since they experience a sadness and disappointment so disturbing, in fact, that they are definitely unhappy. Furthermore, what they absolutely need has to be something *different* from the satisfaction of their well-known desires, since they already have that satisfaction, most of the time. So what is it they would want so much to obtain, and that they would surely like to get themselves determined on trying to obtain, if they could?

The following facts may already suggest a possible answer to that question. It has often been observed, for instance, that the more a person is determined on living a certain kind of life, the more that person is happy when actually living that very life (and the more unhappy, of course, when constantly failing to do so). But what, exactly, does a person's determination *change* in the situation? This, at least, is different: when I am *determined* on obtaining the satisfaction of my most pressing desires (and employ myself in finding the means to obtain it), and when it happens that my desires are in fact fulfilled, I may be under the impression, at the same time, that the acts *of my own determined will* are also fulfilled. ("Willing" something, even with a certain determination, is also, in a sense, only "expecting" something, since I cannot say that I have *always* succeeded in doing or obtaining what I actually *had* the will to do or to obtain.) In fact, I can even be under the impression that I, myself, am much more *present* in the acts of my own determined will, than in the desires — even the more intense ones — that I happen (only) to experience.

Because of this impression of "presence", one can understand that what satisfies and pleases me the most, when I am living happily, is much less the fact that my needs or desires are fulfilled, than the fact that *my own* will gets realized; or that fact that I am obtaining what I, *myself*, am presently determined on obtaining. For the same reason, one could also understand that the people whose desires are all pretty well satisfied can *nevertheless* feel quite unhappy, when they cannot obtain what their own *selves* happen to be set on obtaining. Although that kind of impression is not felt by everybody, it still is true that many people are convinced (or behave as if they were) that the fact that they have become happy has occurred "in response to" their own acts of the will, or their own efforts and expectations. It sometimes happens that they are convinced, for example, that the realization of their determined acts of the will did not occur out of *pure chance*, or because of the efficiency of their own will and efforts, but rather (and mostly) because their own *selves* were somehow involved, or even at stake. They are spontaneously convinced that this realization could very well have *not* occurred (in spite of all their efforts), but that it nevertheless did occur, and for the reason that *they* wanted it, were determined on obtaining it, and were hoping for it...

The same persons don't always dare to consider seriously the foregoing interpretation of their experience, nor to explain the latter or talk about it in such an explicit manner, since it is a kind of experience which appears to them as much too extravagantly or naively self-centered. Yet they do agree that this interpretation is a reasonably good expression of what would constitute the most important and valuable component of the happiness they feel, when their own acts of the will are actually realized. (It is also true, however, that they rather prefer to talk about their luck, their good fortune, or their "lucky star", instead...)

Other facts would also suggest a similar interpretation. Many people don't seem to be really satisfied when noticing that their desires and acts of the will are regularly fulfilled — automatically fulfilled, as it were. What they desire but seems to be lacking at certain moments, is that they *themselves* had something to do — something really *active* and *indispensable* — about the way in which their life actually unfolded itself, no matter how happily it happened to do so. It is as if even the most enjoyable of lives couldn't but leave them indifferent, when all they had to do was to take it in and enjoy it, while nonchalantly stretching their limbs ...and yawning. What these people would actually want, what they at times cannot help but wanting above all, is to know that their "happy" life is not only the result of the simple satisfaction of desires they never even chose to have or to feel, but also (and more importantly) the result of the fact that they were living the life which they *themselves* wanted to live, and towards which, therefore, they had chosen to have a truly *personal* interest.

In other words, the active and indispensable contribution that these people would want to bring in (to their happy life) would be that of their free and personal choice of such a life, that is, a choice which would enable them to be present in it themselves, or to be living it *personally*. Should they ever succeed in living such a life, then obviously it is their own *personal* will and interest which would be satisfied (not only the desires they happened to have!), and their own active and personal expectation which would then be fulfilled. The resulting happiness would also be a more personal one, being the happiness of their person *itself.* And since all these people would be living the life they personally wanted to live, they would be living at least "fundamentally" happy, and could never be too seriously frustrated, or hurt, by the fact that some of their desires still remained more or less painfully unsatisfied. (The phrase "fundamentally happy", so far adopted, thus turns out to mean: "personally happy".)

Another fact apparently points in the same direction. Among the people who want to live an actively and personally happy life, there are some who would also want that life not to be any kind of life, but the *best possible* one. For example, they couldn't imagine themselves living happily in trying to set up the most complete collection of various match books; nor even choosing to get personally interested in such a trivial life (were it the condition, in fact, for living a personally happy life). There are also those who are struck by the "insignificance" of a life dedicated to sports or pure mathematics, or even, finally, to space research, politics, social work, or to any "useless" form of education... On the other hand, it happens to many people who have become suddenly convinced of never being able to live a *truly* happy life, to adopt the kind of life which would at least appear to be the best, or less insignificant (rather than the kind which might contain a greater number of pleasant moments), but only to discover afterwards, little by little, that they are now much happier than they would have believed, or more fundamentally and personally happy, in any case... It is also a fact that in such moments, the "insignificance" of their life becomes much less striking.

What is there to think, in the end, of all those demands concerning a happy life? Are they extravagant and deceptive, or reasonable and somehow quite relevant? In any case, they sometimes do seem to express, in various ways, the widely shared desire to live a life which would be that of one's own person *itself.* But if so, how, then, could that particular desire be fulfilled?

A "personally" happy life

The preceding section has brought out the fact that many people feel they have to impose certain conditions for what would be a truly happy life. First, that they lived a life which they, themselves, wanted above all to live; and that they also knew, somehow, that if the circumstances could very well have prevented them from living such a life but *did not* do so, it wasn't out of pure *chance*, but rather because *they*, themselves, were concerned, and *personally* wanted to live that kind of life. (Such a condition may appear quite extravagant, but it remains a fact that people often require it, without always realizing that they do.) Furthermore, a truly happy life should not be passively "received", but should be such, on the contrary, that it could not possibly be lived without one's personal and indispensable contribution. And finally, it shouldn't be just any kind of life — an insignificant one! —, but a life which would be, as far as possible, the best one.

These people haven't chosen, of course, to *require* such conditions. Yet it does seem that no other kind of life could really satisfy the desire they feel, at certain moments, for a kind of happiness which could be called the happiness of the person *itself.* Many of them keep wondering what they could do, in practice, to become able to live that kind of life; or what it is that would have to happen to them, sooner or later, so that they became able to do so, and therefore to live a life which would be at least "fundamentally" happy. It so happens, however, that an answer to these questions is already contained, implicitly, in the conditions for the possibility of all *free* choices, already described in the previous section. It will now become clear, in fact, that if those conditions were actually realized, they would enable anyone to live the kind of life that many people seem to yearn for, in order to live more "personally" happy.

Let us suppose, then, that Richard suddenly feels that it is expected of him, as it were, that he gave himself a certain consideration, or respect, for someone else. That could have happened, for example, when John — one of his neighbors — had requested his help for a couple of hours. Strongly disinclined, Richard hesitated. (After all, he too had a lot of things to do!) He was about to refuse his neighbor's request when he realized, all of a sudden, that he would certainly be lacking in consideration towards John — towards his *person* —, if he chose to refuse. As for John, it could very well be that he expected no particular consideration from Richard, when he simply asked for his help. If so, everything could still have occurred as it did, for Richard. (It isn't that John would have been totally indifferent to any consideration coming from Richard: the reason might be that he just hadn't thought about that, when he asked Richard for the *help* he most needed at that moment.)

In any case, if Richard can realize that he would be lacking in consideration towards John if he refused to help him, it is no doubt because he also has the feeling that it is already expected from him (as it were) that he gave himself a certain consideration for John — a consideration which John himself might not be expecting right now, but which he *could* expect at any moment. After a while, Richard actually chooses to give himself the consideration, for John, which he feels is "in any case" expected from him. And to do that *effectively*, he starts *helping* John. (His choice may be considered a free and personal one, since the conditions for the possibility of free choices — as described in the preceding section — were indeed present.)

One may note, here, that so long as Richard is busy helping his neighbor *out of a truly personal consideration for him*, he is living the life he *personally* wants to live, and a life which he couldn't possibly be living if he, himself, were not producing his free, indispensable, and "considerate" contribution to it. As we have already observed, if Richard had not felt this expectation concerning his own consideration towards John, he could still have *helped* him, of course, but only out of some inclination or fear, or only because of his desire to avoid unpleasant consequences, or possible regrets. In other words, Richard would have been inevitably driven by his stronger or more recent desires (nothing necessarily disappointing or regrettable about that!), and living a passive life, rather than a personally active one. But if he actually felt that expectation, and finally chose to act out of a true consideration for John — thereby giving himself a personal interest in his person —, then he would have *really* become interested in that person. (He could have said, for instance, that he was interested in *being* interested in that person, and therefore in *continuing* to be interested in — and to help — that same person.)

During those moments, Richard is thus living a kind of life which certainly interests him, yet can only do so if (and when) he alone — or out of himself *alone* — makes himself *become* personally interested in it. But it is precisely this personally active component of the life he is now living, which makes that life a "fundamentally" happy one, and a *personally* happy one at that. (One could also note that the *other* persons — in this case John — need not necessarily appreciate Richard's consideration and interest, and need not even notice that the help they receive is being offered, above all, out of *consideration* for them...)

It is now easier to see how the life of a person, in such cases, is also the "best possible" life. Both subjectively *and* "objectively". To choose is indeed to prefer, and one always prefers the best to the worst, or to that which, in the present circumstances, would be a lesser good. So persons like the one considered above are happy, since they are living the life which they themselves choose and *prefer* to live, and is *therefore* the best possible one.

It is a common belief that any thing, behavior, or act, is "good" (or a "value"), if someone is "positively" interested in it, that is, if someone wants it, desires it, loves it, and so on. And it is "bad" (or a "disvalue"), if someone is "negatively" interested in it, that is, if someone hates it, is annoyed or repelled by it, and so on. When no one is either positively or negatively interested in a thing, that thing is neither good nor bad. It is indifferent, it has no value at all (either positive or negative). In other words, things and acts are good or bad, or they are positive or negative values, only when *other* beings have positive or negative feelings, or inclinations, concerning them. (French fries would be neither good nor bad, if no one ever loved them or hated them.) But that is to say that *in themselves*, things and acts are neither good nor bad, neither the best nor the worst. Their goodness or badness are "subjective", depending *only* on the "subjectivity" of other beings — a subjectivity which varies in time, frequency, and number. Positive and negative values are therefore not only subjective, but also relative.

One could ask if there are any "objective" values. Are there things or acts which would be "objectively" good or bad? And what would *that* mean? What could be the *meaning* of a thing being good or bad "in itself", that is, independently of the desires or the interests — the "subjectivity" — of other beings? It seems that if there ever were such a thing as the "objectivity" of any particular goodness, then it would have to be something which included the *subjectivity* of the beings confronted with that goodness, and not something which would *exclude* it. In other words, an "objectively" good thing would have to be both objectively *and* subjectively good. But how would that be possible? Fortunately, we happen to have a case at hand. Up to this point, the things and acts we considered as subjectively good or bad were the ones with regard to which we *already* felt a desire (to have them or to perform them), or in which we *already* had an interest. They were desires or interests we never gave to ourselves, and about which we never even *thought* of choosing or deciding to have them or not. But what about the interests we could *freely* give to ourselves, simply by freely choosing to have them? For example, what about "consideration" —

a *personal* one — for other persons? (Or all the other types of "interests" in the persons themselves, such as respect, care, solicitude, or concern?)

Let us consider, for a moment, the case of a person who freely chose (and therefore preferred) to get itself personally interested, whenever possible, in living with an enduring and sincere consideration for all other persons. The ensuing life would of course be the best possible one for that person, and for any other person who would have freely chosen to *prefer* the same kind of life. In other words, it would be "subjectively" the best life — just as beer is "subjectively" the best drink, at a certain moment, for the people who choose that particular drink in preference to all others. But that person could have noticed — as many people do — that he or she had the conviction, even *before* choosing, that such a life already "deserved" that they, themselves, freely chose and preferred to get themselves personally interested in it (instead of choosing not to do do); or that it was a kind of life which was already "worthy" of their personal consideration and interest.

It seems quite natural to think that things like fresh air, mathematics, or interesting movies, are only *subjectively* "good" (or "valuable", or "the best"); and only when someone *happens* to desire them, or to prefer them to anything else. (If we happened to dislike them, we could still call them "good", but only when we thought they were the means to obtain something *else* which we already desired.) If we happened to feel no interest at all in things of that kind, we wouldn't seriously think that *they* nevertheless deserved our interest. But a life which is accompanied by a constant consideration for all persons, is something which can be said to be *objectively* good (or an *objective* value), at least for persons who really feel that such a life somehow "deserves" their *personal* consideration and interest. That particular conviction is indeed about the fact that, independently of the desires a person already had for that kind of life, or of the interest a person already felt in it — and even independently of the strong aversion a person actually felt to that kind of life —, it still deserved, *itself*, the freely chosen consideration and interest of any person.

The foregoing observations can help us portray, more exactly, the seldom described *meaning* of words or phrases like "good", "objectively good", and "deserve". We usually consider things to be "good" when they play a part in fulfilling a desire we happen to have for *a feeling of enjoyment*. (There are many kinds of enjoyment: pleasure, contentment, serenity, wonder, bliss, ravishment, and so on.) In a sense, enjoyment is actually the only thing we consider as being "good", since what we finally desire, or what we happen to be really interested in, is always one of the various kinds of *enjoyment*. But if we happened to have no desire at all for feelings of enjoyment, then we could hardly ever think of considering enjoyment itself as something "good". However, we do consider many things as being "good" — like money, companionship, walks, music, or sunsets —, but that is only because these things or activities participate, in all sorts of ways, in bringing about a feeling of enjoyment. Other things or activities are also called "good", even when they give rise to "bad" feelings of unpleasantness or pain — like hard work, displeasing surroundings, asking for help —, but always provided that they are necessary means to obtain a particular satisfaction and enjoyment.

We then have desires for feelings of enjoyment, or an interest in them. We could say, about enjoyment, that it is a "subjectively" good thing, in the sense that it is good only because it is the object of an interest that *we* happen to have in it. Enjoyment doesn't really appear to be a good thing "itself", that is, when we only consider what *it* is. Things which participate in making us experience a certain enjoyment don't appear, for that reason, as being "themselves" good. About these subjectively good things — even about enjoyment —, we wouldn't say that *they* really deserved to be the objects of our desires or interests. Nor would we say that, simply because of what *they* are, we "should" desire them, or at least try to get ourselves interested in *them*. There are things, however, about which we sometimes feel that they certainly *deserve* to be the objects of our own interest, and apparently only because of what they are. That would be the case, for instance, when we are in the presence of persons who are claiming something as a *right*. If we then happen to feel the moral obligation of giving them what they claim — while also feeling that they actually do have that right —, we might have the further conviction that they have the right, in fact, to the consideration (for them) which would be presently required for us to respond appropriately. In other words, we might notice that what their right (and our obligation) *primarily* concerns is not the thing they are claiming, but our own consideration for them, and therefore our own freely chosen and personal interest in *them*.

In such cases, we could even feel — as we occasionally do — that it is quite normal and not at all surprising, that these people should have the *right* to our personal consideration and interest, and simply because of what *they* are. In fact, that would be at the very moment when they actually appeared to us as beings who *deserved* our consideration and interest. We would then know — from experience — that what these people are, more typically, is what we mean when we call them "persons". And also what we finally mean, when we say that it is the *person* of each of these people — *not* their different and variable qualities, capacities, or performances —, who "deserves" our consideration and interest.[7]

It may be noted, here, that the term "deserves" apparently gets its meaning from the content of the following experiences. Contrary to enjoyment (or to things which participate in bringing about any feeling of that kind), persons are *apt* (or have "what it takes") to become the objects of any real interest, or consideration, which other persons would *freely* make themselves have. But since persons cannot automatically induce, in other persons, such a *freely* acquired (and truly personal) interest in them — as the presence or even the mere thought of many kinds of things can actually trigger off our interest in the enjoyment these things might cause us to experience —, yet persons definitely do have the *aptitude* to become objects of freely acquired interests in them; and since the other persons who actually get themselves *really* interested in them usually experience the kind of enjoyment that can be expected from the satisfaction of the interest one has in such "objects", it seems that those facts can be described by saying that persons "deserve" that other persons got themselves interested in *them*.

Precisely because persons are *apt* to become the objects of the freely produced interest of other persons, their presence — whether "in person" or simply in thought — actually *enables* these others to make them become objects of their personally chosen interest in them. In other words, they enable these other persons to make *them* become, if they should freely choose to do so, their own "subjective" good. But since this aptitude of theirs doesn't at all depend on the persons who do choose to make them become their subjective good, but only on what *they* are, these other persons can, and often do recognize, in their present *subjective* good, something that is also *objectively* good (or that is good "in *itself*"). On the contrary, "impersonal" things or activities — like appetizing food, wonderful sunsets, or fascinating

[7] There is nothing particularly *mystical* about all that! Many people — ordinary people, or even ...well, *other* people — actually do have these feelings and experiences in their everyday lives, whether in buses, cafeterias, workshops or offices, even though they hardly ever have the time, or the capacity (or the desire) to *describe* them.

mathematics — cannot be seen as things which, being what they are, *enable* us to make them become our subjective good. Our own (subjective) *desire*, not food itself, nor sunsets or mathematics themselves, is what makes these impersonal things become (or appear?) good, while actually leaving them as they are "objectively", or "in themselves", that is, neither good nor bad.

Looking back, now, at the question of whether or not living with a constant personal consideration for other people — and therefore with a constant interest in *them* — is a life which could be both subjectively *and* objectively good, one can come to the conclusion that the answer is yes. Since feelings of enjoyment seem to be the only thing that is desired and therefore subectively good, the life we are now considering is not subjectively good. That life is only a process, not a feeling of enjoyment. But such a process is of a kind which usually gives rise to particular feelings of enjoyment, and, for that reason, can be considered as partaking, to a certain extent, of the goodness of that enjoyment. And since persons are the only objectively good "things", the same life is not, as a process or activity, an objectively good thing. It is nevertheless a necessary means for persons to get themselves *related* to the objective (or "deserving") goodness of other persons, and may therefore be considered — as it often is — as an objectively good life.

It is finally obvious that the people who give themselves a personal consideration for other persons and thus get themselves interested in them, are not only living a fundamentally happy life, but also a life which is quite the opposite of an "insignificant" one. They could notice indeed that the persons they are now interested in happen to have, only because of what they are, all that is needed to enable them to get interested, out of *themselves alone*, in *them*. On the contrary, all other things — including enjoyment itself — are in themselves insignificant, since it is only the desires experienced by people or animals, which make them become (or appear) interesting. (Some people are repeatedly struck by this insignificance of all things *themselves*, of life in general, and even of their own reasonably happy life, the result being that they often become deeply depressed.) As for people who would maintain a constant consideration for persons, and therefore a persisting interest in *them* — that is, in something objectively good and not at all insignificant —, one can understand how (and why) these people would be living an objectively interesting life, a truly significant one, and — in spite of any unpleasant or even painful moments — an at least fundamentally *happy* life.

Isn't there something unbearably insignificant, however, in the very fact that we are all deeply immersed in an existence where, in order to live a happy life, we would have to live "outside" of ourselves, always having *the others* as our only objects of interest? (It isn't guaranteed, of course, that having *ourselves* as our only object of interest would turn out to be a much less insignificant kind of happy life...) What could actually be missing, here? No doubt nothing at all, for many people. For others, however, this unrolling of a personally happy life — be it a very happy one — sometimes appears as "mechanically conditional", and therefore insignificant. These others could say, for instance: "It is a fact that I often *need* to live "personally" happy, and that all I would have to do in order to fulfill such a powerful desire, is to get myself personally interested in other persons. I know, because I've done it often enough... But what I *don't* know, however, is what would still have to happen, so that I wouldn't any more find my life, or life in general, so sadly insignificant. What *is* it that I desire but doesn't seem to happen or to come, or that I just can't seem to recognize?".

The probability is that only the people who experience such a puzzling and apparently objectless desire, could appreciate whether or not the following proposition is at all relevant. Could it be that, besides wanting to live a life in which they would be personally interested, or which they would find really significant, these people also needed to have *their own persons* become the objects of a true consideration and interest (and thus become "significant")? Or needed to know, in other words, that other people were personally interested in *their own* persons? Or even to realize not only that they already *had* everything that would be required for others to become personally interested in them, but also, and above all, that others were *in fact* interested in *them*?

Would such a need be the intense desire to be delivered from one's own personal insignificance, by becoming a person who would be living happily not "out of pure chance", but mostly because other persons had finally spotted them, and gotten really interested in them, in their own *persons*. If so, then one could understand that the only life which could be a truly happy one for these people, is a life of *mutual* personal consideration and interest; in other words, a life which would be an *exchange* of freely offered and accepted consideration, and would be an important first step, therefore, towards friendship, or love, between the persons *themselves*.[8] Persons having preferred to live such a life would also consider it as the best possible one, and not in the least bit insignificant or arbitrary.

Justice and the happy life

It has thus appeared that it isn't by pursuing the fulfillment of one's most pressing and persistent desires, that one could succeed in living the happiest possible life, the reason being that a fundamentally happy life can only be the consequence of the fact that a person is living out of a "personal" consideration for others. (Needless to say, any *true* consideration must express itself, whenever possible, by various kinds of appropriate concrete *behavior*.) In any case, all other kinds of life would be the lives of puppets — sometimes very happy ones! —, rather than a freely chosen life, a life in which one would have given himself, or herself, a really personal interest.

That doesn't have to mean that persons should never be in search of the happiest possible life for themselves (or for others), since all that the preceding conclusions assert is this: to be capable of choosing and acting out of themselves alone, and therefore capable of living *freely*, people must absolutely have as a *principal* aim (not the *only* one!) that of maintaining a truly personal consideration for other people. There is nothing really inappropriate or self-defeating, therefore, in wanting to experience the enjoyment which often accompanies the factual unrolling of that kind of life, nor in wanting to live an ever happier life.

It is fortunate, in a sense, that a fundamentally happy life need not *itself* be sought, and that none of us had to make sure, by a constantly renewed choice of occupations and behavior, that he or she will be able to live such a life until the end. A lucid person may easily become aware of the fact, indeed, that we never really *know* if the good consequences which would immediately follow our acts and behavior won't be followed, sooner or later, by totally unexpected consequences which would be much more *harmful* (for the rest of our lives) than would have been the consequences of any *other* act or behavior. It seems that most people have never

---

[8] The need to become the object of the consideration or the interest of other persons could only be satisfied, of course, by persons for whom we *ourselves* have a certain consideration. That need is therefore that of a *mutual* consideration and interest. The *social* relevance and meaning of such a need should appear more clearly in the last section of the present book.

noticed that insurmountable ignorance of ours; or that if they did, they soon forgot about it, or else quickly succeeded in protecting themselves from the paralyzing anxiety it could easily provoke...

One can notice, of course, that some of the worst consequences (like someone having become permanently bedridden?) can also be followed or accompanied by the most extraordinarily *happy* consequences — as for the man who had met, when he was a "hopeless" case at the hospital, the nurse who subsequently became "the love of his life"; or for the woman who, in similar circumstances and only to "forget" her unbearable situation, "wrote" on cassette what she thought were novels of the poorest kind, and yet became the most cherished (and visited) novelist of her generation. It still remains a fact, however, that we cannot but remain totally in the dark as to whether, as a consequence of our acts and omissions (and of everything else!), the rest of our lives, as a whole, will be rather happy, or mostly miserable.

Such a fact need not worry anyone to any serious extent, if it is also a fact that the fundamentally happy future of persons — of people having the capacity to choose and to act *freely* — doesn't depend on the *consequences* of their present acts and behavior only, but essentially on the personal consideration which they would freely *maintain*, in the future, towards other persons (while trying to express it, all along, by means of their immediate acts and behavior). There would be no cause to worry, in particular, about the distant consequences, for one's future happiness, of acts required by *justice*. On the contrary. By coercing persons into choosing and acting freely, moral obligations of justice enable them to act out of a personal consideration for others, and therefore to live a life in which they had a *personal* interest, that is, a fundamentally happy life.

Persons who had chosen to become and also to *remain* personally concerned about justice, about their own consideration for others, would thus have nothing to fear as regards the fundamental happiness of their future. (They could at least notice that it doesn't matter much, in fact, whether their concern for *concrete* justice often prevents them from adopting a more pleasant or enviable life style — can they really be sure that they *could have* adopted such a life style anyway, if they remember how unexpectedly accidents happen? —; or whether justice sometimes requires, indirectly, that they simply endured the painful unsatisfaction of a present desire, since they can still continue to live a life of true consideration for the others, and therefore to enjoy the happiness of a life in which they were *personally* interested.) By the very fact that they are living happily in doing so, the same persons often contribute to the *fundamental* happiness of *other* persons, particularly to that of the destitute and the castoff, if it is actually true that many of these persons suffer much more from the lack of consideration, or even from the *contempt* of the others, than from the painful consequences of their *behavior* or *omissions*.

Should we think that, in order to make sure that we could live a fundamentally happy life, we had better seek our happiness only in being "considerate" towards the others? Must one somehow give up one's own happiness in favor of that of the others, in order to regain it with a better hold on it? (These questions imply that one hasn't lost sight of his or her own happiness...) The answer, of course, is yes, provided that the other persons *themselves* became "objects" of a truly *personal* interest. There is always the risk that one might not be "personally" *present* within his or her interest in the other persons, the latter being then merely considered as parts of a set of "means" (totally indifferent *in themselves*!) for a happier life. Yet, having a real consideration for other persons is not *necessarily* incompatible with naturally keeping an eye on (and an interest in) one's own happiness. So when things are not all that clear, the practical question would not be this one: "Do I have *enough* interest in those other people, or am I only interested in a happy life?" Nor even this one: "Will I ever succeed in playing this little game correctly?" The question would rather be something like the following one: "What shall I *now* choose: a) to find happiness *in addition to* living with consideration for others, or b) to do my best to be happy — as I will often be unless I'm really unlucky —, without worrying *too much* about other persons?" (Such a question could only come up, of course, if one really *had* a choice.)

That question might indeed be more to the point, since it seems quite natural to think, at times, that we should all spend quite a bit of our time and energy on the various "things" of the world we live in, so as to better increase our own chances for a happy future. Shouldn't we acquire the best possible skill or competence in some craft, profession, or preferred occupation? Isn't it reasonable that one should take measures to meet one's appropriate companion, and sometimes the means to retain his or her love or friendship? And if one would rather live off other people, shouldn't he or she work hard in order to be at the right spot at the right time, or to win the favor of the most influential people? On the other hand, it still remains a hard fact that we never have any reliable *knowledge* concerning the more distant consequences of our own activities — consequences which could very well enhance our chances of a happy life, but also destroy them, and perhaps forever.

So if, in spite of that fact, we still had to do *something* about our happy future — whether as a long-range project, or only as the present circumstances would require —, it seems that our *primary* concern shouldn't be to engage in any definite kind of *outward* activity, but in one which could be immediately and happily produced (and maintained) in our own selves, at the same time as we producing *all sorts* of outward activities (for example, working, in a factory, a hospital, a grocery store; or making love, having a discussion, working on a particular project, or trying to get a better job). If that immediate or "inner" production were impossible, then the people whose most pressing desire demanded that they engaged in some definite outward type of happy life — and in no other! — could only count on an extraordinary luck, in order to experience long periods of happiness, if only because of the inevitable and often incorrigible *reversals* in the situations and dependability of our world itself.

If, however, the happiness of the *living* person — not that of the purely passive one — can only be the spontaneous repercussion of the fact that he or she is living a freely chosen life of consideration for other persons, then the primary concern of any person, regarding his or her long-lasting happiness, should obviously be to take up only those outward activities which could be natural *expressions* of their own consideration towards others, or could at least be produced and perceived as *not* being expressions of contempt towards these others. One should always expect, therefore, that any determinate plan of life, just as any short-term project, would have to be sooner or later modified or even abandoned, because of unforeseeable changes in the situations, yet without one's freely chosen attitude of consideration (for the persons themselves) having for all that to be dropped or to disappear; or without one becoming actually unable to find *other* concrete occasions of expressing the same freely chosen attitude. So the personal happiness of anyone — the happiness which spontaneously accompanies these "considerate" activities, no matter which — would never have to disappear, nor even to lose any of its particular flavor.

Even if obligations of justice can often require that we simply renounced the satisfaction of certain desires, and gave up certain projects or activities which were meant to ensure that satisfaction, they could never thereby threaten the *personal* happiness of anyone. On the contrary, by demanding concrete expressions of consideration towards others, these obligations are just as many occasions for us, as persons immersed in our world, to regenerate our *personal* existence, and therefore to live a more fundamentally happy life. And so it seems that our many particular obligations of justice wouldn't be constraints imposed on the *happiness* of our persons, but real possibilities for us to live personally happy, in spite of the fact that we remain totally in the dark as to whether the more distant consequences of our outward activities will mostly favor the satisfaction of our desires, or rather hinder that same satisfaction. In the last section of this book, an attempt will be made to see how governmental projects and policies *could* take into account this *personally* happy life of each and every one of the citizens, and this insurmountable ignorance of the long-term consequences of any concrete activity or behavior.

6. WHAT COULD CITIZENS EXPECT FROM THEIR GOVERNMENTS?

What *can* be expected from any government? Even in our more democratic countries, what could the citizens expect from their political rulers who possess, according to a widespread belief, a power much greater than that of any other members or groups of their society? The richer citizens not having yet acquired the noticeable habit of turning towards their governments for things concerning their everyday lives, the question may be considered, here, as regarding above all the underpriviledged citizens, as well as those who belong to the so-called middle class.

However, this question doesn't mean to discover what the citizens could expect from their present government, nor even what they might have the *right* to expect from that government. More exactly, the question is the following one: "What are the kinds of intervention that the citizens could expect, in a fairly realistic way, from a government which would not only be 'well disposed' towards each one of them, but also have the actual *capacity* to fulfill such expectations?". The solution to that problem is constantly sought, of course, by those of the political rulers who are more interested in the living conditions of the citizens — or in the citizens *themselves* — than in the possession and enjoyment of "supreme" power. But the main results of their inquiry have always remained, up to now, mere objects of endless debate...

As should become clear in the following pages, the answer to that question is already contained, at least implicitly, in the apparently unreasonable expectations of the citizens with regard to their government, and in the results of the present research concerning the *main* objects of 1) the widespread desire for justice, and 2) the even more universal pursuit of a happy life.

The expected improvement

That which most citizens expect from a "well disposed" government is that it reduced, by means of laws and *effective* sanctions, the number of acts of injustice which many citizens force others to suffer, and also supplied with an indispensable aid those whom the circumstances (or injustice) had deprived of a decent well-being. In other words, the majority of citizens expect that such a government *improved* the conditions of life in their own society, thereby promoting the well-being of each one of its members. The cause of this spontaneous expectation is obviously the no less spontaneous pursuit of a happy life, a pursuit which the citizens hope that it will be successful not only for themselves, but also, as a rule, for all the members of their society.

Because of the supposedly "supreme" force of the government, many citizens believe that the latter certainly *could* improve the situation, at least for the greater number. Above all, they believe it could put a stop, with an ever greater efficiency, to all that which some do, and which keeps others from pursuing and attaining a reasonably happy life. After all, isn't that simply a matter of organization, method, and strategy? Couldn't the government identify the activities or the kinds of behavior which should absolutely be forbidden (or prescribed), so that no citizen seriously hindered any other? Aren't these hindrances actually indicated, at least implicitly, by the "rights of the citizens" which already appear — and quite conspicuously — in their country's *Constitution*? Isn't it a fact, also, that the purpose of these rights is precisely to promote the most *efficient* pursuit, by all citizens, of a decently happy life, that is, a pursuit which would never be restrained by any of the other citizens?

If that is in fact the particular improvement that most citizens expect from their governments, it does seem, however, that very few have realized the *impossibility*, for *any* government, of achieving such a task. But that impossibility itself actually comes from the fact that most citizens are convinced that there is a *necessary* connection between a happy life, and a certain number of very definite activities. (You just *won't* live happily, if you don't succeed in doing or obtaining *this* or *that* thing!...) As a matter of fact, many citizens imagine a happy life as a succession of the precise kinds of enjoyable moments they most wanted to live, no one (or nothing) ever being allowed to stop them, therefore, from doing the precise things they would have to do in order to live such a life.

People don't seem to have noticed that if such a conception of the happy life and of the "indispensable" means to it were valid, then no one could ever *know* whether such and such a government law or policy would actually *improve* the situation of the citizens, or make it *worse*. Haven't the citizens ever noticed, for example, that if the government had not imposed this particular law, then surely they, as a consequence, would never have gone to such and such a place, and would therefore never have done such and such a thing, and could never *have been* the victims, then, of the particular events which made it impossible for them to live a truly happy life? [9] On the other hand, it is also true that they can never know whether they wouldn't have been the victims of still more disastrous events which they simply *could not* have suffered, in fact, if the government had *not* imposed that same law... (One could obviously make similar observations concerning the "happier" consequences of government laws.)

It should be noted, however, that what the majority of the citizens mostly fear is not the fact that they might be momentarily hindered — even for quite a while — from living what they particularly wanted to live, and therefore to be hindered, for *a certain* period of time, from living a sufficiently happy life. (One should expect such "accidents" to happen, even painful ones.) What they fear above all, whether they were aware of it or not, is the prospect of becoming incapable, for *the rest* of their days, of doing what they would *have* to do, in order to live a reasonably happy life. Some people even fear the possibility of never being able to stop *wanting* to live a *really* happy life — not just a "reasonably" happy one—, and yet of never being able, for the rest of their days, to find the means to *live* that kind of life. (Such a fear isn't experienced *only* by the underpriviledged and the poor...) But most citizens rather fear certain well-known incapacities they could easily inherit from the

[9] As examples of the so-called perverse effects of government laws on *many* people, one can think of higher income tax, unemployment, reduced welfare allowances. But one could also think of the painful accidents which individuals might suffer for having *obeyed* these laws. (A family went to a less expensive place for the holidays, and one of the children died of a car accident at *that* place...)

behavior of other citizens, and which they believe could make them become *forever* incapable of living a reasonably happy life.

It then seems quite natural that most citizens had the tendency to expect, from their government, that it *stepped in*, with its organized "supreme" power, and made sure that all the citizens would have the necessary concrete means to preserve, to increase, or to recuperate their "indispensable" capacity to live a happy life until the very end. In any case, many citizens certainly wish that their government at least improved the *general* situation.

However, we have just seen the reason why this kind of improvement is actually impossible, or why this wish cannot be fulfilled. Indeed, for a government to know, before stepping in, whether its own interventions will be followed by a real *improvement* of the situation (rather than by something quite the opposite, like a long and difficult general strike, for example), it would have to know if, precisely because of *that* particular intervention (and no doubt many other "appropriate" ones!), a good majority of the citizens would be able to live a happier life for the rest of their days, or a less unhappy one, at least. But it is obvious that on that subject, the government's ignorance — just as anyone else's — will always be totally insurmountable.

What should we think, then, about the fact that many citizens persist in requiring this impossible improvement from their government? And what should we think about the fact that our political rulers are always ready to *promise* such an improvement of the situation? Could those citizens be so naive, and our political rulers just a bunch of compulsive liars? But could it also be that many of these people have actually felt, at certain moments, that a real improvement of life in our societies should somehow be possible "in spite of everything"? Isn't it obvious, for many, that we should at least *do* something? Or at least *try* to do something? (But then *what*? And *why*?)

Since it is a fact that we never know which concrete, effective, and successive means we would have to take, so as to become able to live a happy life *until the very end*, many people tend to believe — as some actually do believe — that the best thing to do, then, is to stop making plans with *that* particular end in view, and to concentrate, instead, on an *immediately* happy life. To focus, for example, on the well-being of each and every moment, which is surely a much more attainable "happiness"... Even the rights of the others, or our own moral obligations, would have to be respected only when they promised a fairly immediate *well-being*, for what would be the point in doing anything unpleasant, or in avoiding any pleasant thing, if we simply don't know whether the *consequences* of our acts or omissions, for the rest of our lives, will be happy ones, or very painful ones. Wouldn't it be more sensible, or more rational and practical, to pursue only our *immediate* satisfactions and enjoyment? (As for the harms caused to others, who knows if, considering *all* their consequences, these others might not live much more happily, until the end, than if they had never suffered those particular harms?...)

For many people, this logic — an undoubtedly strict one — is impossible to live with. Even though they acknowledge their insurmountable ignorance of the consequences of their outward acts, these people just can't get rid of their "fundamental" fear, which impels them not only to act in spite of that ignorance, but even to consider themselves responsible, at times, for certain *immediate* consequences of their behavior. Nor could they persist very long in ignoring the sensitivity they have, concerning the rights of the others, and their own social obligations. In addition, there is the fact that many underpriviledged or "incapable" people — very poor candidates for a happy life? — actually succeed, without violating anyone's rights, in living a life apparently happier, or more serene (and in any case less frustrating) than that of the richer and more capable citizens. Could it be that respecting the rights of the others were never an obstacle to a truly happy life, and that in spite of our ignorance of the positive or negative consequences of our acts and behavior, such a respect were even a means not only to act both reasonably and happily, but also to improve the social situation *itself*?

Having the answer to that question would no doubt represent a great advantage, especially since our democratic societies are more sensitive than ever to the "respect of the persons", and not too worried, as it seems, about the consequences which the "perverse" effects of one's *concrete* respect of these rights might actually have, in the future, on his or her own chances for a happy life. (And on anyone else's chances, for that matter.) But what, then, would be the main object of that particular sensitivity, and the reason for this rather strange absence of worry, concerning the possibility of such "perverse" effects?

A possible guide: the "better"

There would be no sense in doing any particular thing — or in refraining from doing any particular thing — if what one wanted above all is to increase one's own chances (or anyone else's chances) of living a life which, until the very end, would be more happy than unhappy. Indeed, we can never know in advance whether the long-term consequences of our successive acts or omissions might not condemn us to a permanently *unhappy* life. So how are we to understand the fact that many people — some of them quite aware of that possibility — are convinced that we should nevertheless *do* something, at least *certain* things, or at least take into account *certain* consequences? Such a conviction can hardly be said to be consistent, but one might ask whether it couldn't somehow *become* reasonable. If, in fact, we were capable of acting sensibly (and freely?), what is it, then, that we would particularly have to set our sights on and pay attention to, since it certainly couldn't be the unpredictable effects of our acts and omissions, on anyone's happy or unhappy future?

It seems that what we would have to aim at, as consequences, has to be something much more *immediate* than anyone's happy *future*. Even if someone knew that it's no use worrying about a happy future, the very fact of aiming at that more immediate something would still have to enable him or her, in some way, *not* to actually worry about that — or not up to the point, at least, of becoming totally unable to aim at that immediate something. Moreover, the fact of simply aiming at such an object must consist in already *attaining* it in some way (and also *knowing* that), for what motive could one otherwise have in aiming at it, if he or she believed they could never know whether or not they had actually attained it? But what kind of object could that be? Can one even imagine what could thus enable anyone to act reasonably, and unhindered by the quite natural fear of an unhappy *future*?

There is, in fact, a solution to that problem, a solution whose elements are suggested by some of our own experiences. Let us consider, for example, a citizen (or a political ruler!) who has decided to do, in the present circumstances, what he feels would be "the better", coming from him. (Many people do let themselves be guided by such a feeling, more or less consciously, especially when the circum–stances are very complicated, or when the consequences of any act or omission are too difficult to appreciate and compare.) That citizen may even be quite aware of the fact that he doesn't know at all *why* such and such an activity would be "the better", coming from him, but he still "feels" that that is so. In other words, he doesn't worry too much about the possibly *unhappy* consequences of following such a feeling, perhaps realizing that he would have to worry just as much about the consequences of any *other* activity. In any case, his principal aim is not a happy life for himself or for others, but simply to do what he feels would be "the better".

One could notice, here, that when that citizen decides to do such and such a thing because he feels it would be the "better" thing to do, it isn't that he is persuaded that it is the thing *itself* (or the doing of it) which is "the better". Upon reflection, he could notice that what is more immediately "the better" is that he *decided*, and decided *himself*, to do what he felt would (then) be "the better". So the better "thing" to "do" is not the production of a thing or activity, but the "production" of a decision, of an act of the will. If, for example, that citizen felt that "the better", for the moment, was that he concentrated his efforts on eliminating unemployment (rather than armed robbery), one could say that he actually *did* "the better", even though unemployment still existed (or had even increased!) after three years of hard work. For the "better" thing to do was to *want* to make unemployment disappear, to want to make *efforts* to that end, and *not* (above all) to *make it* disappear. How, indeed, could it be otherwise, since the act of the will — or the intent — directly depends on each and everyone one of us, while its concrete realization, in the world, depends on a great number of things most of which we are not even aware of, and which are totally *out of our control*? We have all noticed quite often, even for the most ordinary things, that having the *will* to do a certain thing is *not* (always) having the *power*, or capacity, to *do* that thing... When "the better" is concerned, it does seem that having the will to do it already consists, in a real an immediate sense, in doing it.

How could that be? In *which* sense? Some people insist on saying that "the better" is *itself* what we should want to do, and that the will to do "the better" is itself the better will, if only because it wills "the better". Of course, that might simply mean that "the better" is not something that is willed because of the *advantages* one might obtain by willing it (like increasing one's chances for a happier life, for example). But that doesn't tell us what one actually wills, when willing "the better". To find out why an act of the will could be considered as being the "better" thing to do, one might perhaps try to find out what happens, more precisely, when someone "feels" it would be "better" — just plain "better"? — to want to do such and such a thing, rather than *not* wanting to do it.

We could easily observe, on certain occasions, that when we feel that such and such a thing would be the "better" thing to do, we also happen to feel we would be totally unable, at that moment, to *refrain* from willing to do that "better" thing, without *thereby* becoming totally indifferent to the situation certain persons are in, or being somewhat lacking in consideration towards those persons themselves. And we could also notice, in such cases, that we would certainly *not* be lacking in consideration towards any person at all, if we decided to *want* to do what seems to be the "better" thing, that is, a thing we couldn't have the *personal* will to do, without that act of the will being accompanied, at least, by a certain amount of consideration for the persons themselves. (It doesn't matter much whether we already knew these persons, or had never met them before.)

It does seem, then, that "the better", even for persons who are not totally aware of it, is that one wanted to act out of consideration, or *with* a certain degree of consideration, for other persons. If persons feel that *this* is, at this moment, "the better" — for example, to set up a new social project, or fight against a parliament bill, or bring help to these people instead of others —, the reason would be that they couldn't refrain from wanting to do those things, right now, without thereby *refusing* to have still more consideration, or a more vivid concern, for other persons. (The "better" is what is often called a moral "value". — The difference between moral values and moral obligations is pointed out in note 6, page 69.) If it happens that the "better" is felt as a moral *obligation* — if people feel *obliged* to do what they also feel would be "the better", or feel it would be *better* to do what they already felt obliged to do —, that is no doubt because they suspect that they could not *want* to do "the better", at this moment, without having to give up, more or less *painfully*, the satisfaction of some of their present desires. In any case, it remains a fact that we couldn't refrain from wanting to do the obligatory "better", without *ourselves* choosing — more consciously and voluntarily — to let ourselves be lacking in consideration for other persons, or to let ourselves have a personal *contempt* towards them.

The best means — if not the only means — to live a meaningful life would thus consist in letting ourselves be guided, in all things, by the feeling we experience of what would be "the better", and in having therefore the constant preoccupation of never lacking in true consideration towards any person. (That would often imply, more positively, that we did things *out of* a personal consideration for others.) Living such a life would also consist, of course, in living freely, since the only way to have a truly personal consideration for others is to choose and decide, out of one's own self *alone,* to have that kind of attitude. And so the persons who maintain that choice and decision always do what they choose *themselves* to do, and therefore what *they* want their own lives to be.

Isn't there something really scary about living a life of constant consideration for other people, however meaningful that could be? What would happen to one's chances for a happy *future*? But then do we ever know what kind of life would actually guarantee a happy future, since we never know whether the consequences of *any* particular present life, concerning our happy future (or that of others), will be mostly positive, *or* mostly negative? As a matter of fact, the persons who could have *more reason* to fear for their future are the ones who are aware of that insurmountable ignorance of ours, and yet never choose to live according to their feeling of what would be "the better", that is, to live out of a true consideration for the others. (Their reasons don't really matter here.) Actually, most of these persons have to live out of a blind hope — still intact and often stimulating —, or else have to be content with living, from day to day, without desiring much of anything (and therefore without having any deep worries about anything).

The situation isn't the same for persons who, although quite aware of this ignorance of ours, have chosen to do "the better", or to live out of a personal consideration for the others, whenever possible. (They had perhaps noticed that, precisely because of that ignorance, they really had nothing to lose anyway.) Such persons are no doubt bound to discover, soon enough, that even though it still happens to them to be seriously annoyed, or disappointed, and even to suffer great pains, yet their fears are less persistent than before, and their worries less disturbing. What they find painful — even very painful — can't make them despairingly unhappy, especially when they remember that they still have the capacity to do what they would *themselves* want to do, namely: maintain the existence of a truly personal consideration for all other persons. And this active and personal pursuit of what is felt as "the better" — a pursuit they could always engage in — also protects them, in fact, against any really paralyzing or oppressive fears concerning their happy future, thus allowing them to live an at least "fundamentally" happy life. ("Fundamentally" happy indeed, since, in spite of everything, their own *persons* are living happily.) The pursuit of "the better" also happens to be, understandably, the best means to live as happy as possible, in a world of constantly unforseeable situations.[10]

A possibility has just been examined: that of "the better", as guide for rational or *meaningful* choices, in a world where no person knows whether the consequences of his or her own actions and omissions will be, on the whole, happy or unhappy ones. But isn't there what might be called a "randomness" (or a "haphazardness") in the actual occurrences of our feelings of what would be "the better"? Isn't there a randomness not only in the occurrences of our thoughts, perceptions, desires, and fears — for no one ever *chooses* to have his or her own thoughts, nor the moment he or she will have them, and never even chooses to have the intention of maintaining such and such a thought —, but also in the fact that we are capable, *or* incapable, of doing a certain thing *without* any personal contempt towards others. Even if all these occurrences were perfectly determined and well ordered, wouldn't it be out of pure chance, *in the end*, that they were *so* determined and ordered?

It is a fact, however, that this randomness of cosmic and human history has the following trait: it now and then *enables* human beings — by pure chance! — to make themselves have, out of themselves *alone*, a certain attitude towards others. But when these human beings actually make themselves have this attitude of consideration towards others, it isn't at all *by pure chance* that they do it, but as a consequence of having had the inevitable choice between doing it *or* not, and of having then *chosen*, out of themselves *alone*, to do just that. Those persons are not

---

[10] One should take into account, here, the painful experience of the many people who *would want* to maintain a constant consideration for all other persons (or to always do the better), yet cannot be sure of *really* wanting that. But *can* one ever be totally satisfied by the authenticity of his or her own consideration — or love — for the others? (Can one be completely satisfied with his or her own *person*?) If not, would this mean that all human beings are condemned never to live as happy *persons*? Is there possibly a kind of salvation, somewhere, for the persons who suffer because of this particular incapacity? Such questions happen to trouble many people (not *all* of them sick!); but dealing with them here would exceed the limits of the present philosophical (and pluralistic) study.

mere spectators — as they could only be for their various thoughts and desires — of a consideration for others which they would have experienced by chance: they are the producers, the *exclusive* producers, of that personal condideration.

Randomness just couldn't cause human beings to have a *personal* consideration towards others. It couldn't, by sheer force, make them have a consideration for others which would be *their own*, since to be their own — not one they would passively experience, even quite pleasantly — it would have to be those human beings themselves, and themselves *alone*, who had made themselves have that particular kind of attitude towards others. (Indeed, what is in question, here, is a "personal" consideration, that is, an attitude about which one would be able to say that it could never have existed (that particular one!), if the persons who now have it were not the *only* beings making it exist, and making it exist both as coming from themselves, and as directed towards other persons themselves.) It still remains a fact, however, that no human beings would be able to make themselves have a *personal* consideration for others, if they were not *by chance* living and conscious, nor having the perceptions, the thoughts, the desires, the feelings of "the better", as well as the capacities and incapacities which they happen *by chance* to have at the moment.

It could thus become obvious for everyone (again by chance) that it is this universal "haphazardness" which determines the thoughts, the desires, the beliefs and convictions of everyone, as also the moments during which one *can* choose to live out of a personal consideration towards others, and therefore *could* live a "personally" happy life. If someone were to ask what it is that this randomness could hold in store for his or her own future (until the end) — for instance, would he or she often have the capacity to choose freely and to live a personally happy life, or would he or she be determined to try, successfully *or* not, to obtain the satisfaction of his or her more pressing desires? —, then he or she could notice (once more by chance!) that a *reassuring* answer would only be possible if it contained a "promise". And such a promise should emanate, of course, from a haphazardness which possessed the equivalent of "personhood", as well as the equivalent of an unfailing "consideration" for all human beings... At any rate, it is clear that in the absence of any such form of actual "promise", only a *totally blind* hopefulness (unaware of itself) could allow human beings, by pure chance, not to be too fearful about their personal or their collective future, and could eventually sustain them — still by pure chance — during their more painful or sorrowful moments.

A possible improvement

Is it possible, therefore, that people were really deluding themselves, when wanting to improve the conditions for a happy life within our societies? In spite of our incapacity to know whether such an such a proposed improvement will be followed by happy *or* by unhappy consequences for each and every one of us (regarding *the rest* of our lives), most people still insist on wanting *something* to be done, at least something which would put an end to the more revolting acts of injustice, and reduce the frequency of harmful behavior. That means, of course, that many are not at all convinced that a true improvement is impossible; on the contrary, they consider themselves quite justified in *hoping*, at least, that many of our efforts can actually contribute, somehow, to the coming of a much better world. But if they *can* have that confident hope, is it because they had perceived the actual possibility of the desired improvement, or at least a sort of "promise" contained in some of their own experiences?

To find the answer to that question, it might be helpful to identify, at first, the particular *kind* of improvement which many people happen to desire (for their own benefit or for that of the others also), when they would like to see an improvement in the observable situations they have more immediately in mind. (We shall be able to observe, in a moment, that in many cases *there is* an improvement which people desire more than any other, and that it happens to be one which can always be quite *reasonably* sought.)

Many people are convinced, for example, that the social condition could certainly be improved if the unemployed found a job; or if the underpriviledged received the surplus, or otherwise the aid which the others could easily offer them. Now this conviction *remains intact* even when these people hear that a number of the former unemployed have suffered, *at work*, accidents which then compelled them to live a life much more "inhuman" than before (and probably for the rest of their days...). The same people still believe that the situation had been improved, in spite of what has happened to those unfortunate persons, that is, in spite of "everything".

It seems that one would have to think, therefore, that their conception of an "improvement" cannot concern *only* (nor even in the first place) the *well-being* of the individuals, or a kind of happy life which they pictured as the simple satisfaction of one's more immediate desires.

One would now have to specify what it is, more exactly, that a society, or the citizens, would especially want to improve when wanting, for example, to create jobs for the unemployed (while feeling, at times, that this would also consist in doing "the better"). Do they think that the improvement is the fact that a desire of the unemployed persons would then be satisfied? If so, is it the job *itself*, that these persons mostly desired, or is it the possibility of finally getting out of a painful situation?... And what could be the most painful for the unemployed persons: the losses suffered up to now, or the anxiety concerning the future, the rest of life itself? But again, if it were this anxiety, would it be focused on the future *losses* — which seem bound to become even worse —, or is it more exactly a particular *fear*, that of persons who suspect they might actually become confirmed in thinking that *they* (as opposed to many others) would be totally *unqualified* to live a decently happy life? (Or that *they* would even be unworthy in fact of living such a life, or of ever becoming able to do so?)

One could indeed notice that the improvement which a great many people more particularly desire is the disappearance, once and for all, of this distinctive fear. More exactly, they would appreciate the presence of whatever could make it disappear, or could at least keep it from presenting itself as a truly *justified* apprehension. As a matter of fact, it often happens that the newly employed persons appreciate much less the fact that they can now satisfy certain desires — and, in *that* sense, live a happier life —, than the fact that the political rulers (or other people in general) have *really* thought that they "had a right" to the desired employment, that they actually "deserved" it as much as others do, and were therefore just as "qualified" *as anyone else* to live a decently happy life.

In other words, it does seem, quite often, that the reason why events and situations are felt as unhappy ones is not so much that they are painful, but that they happen to acquire a particular *meaning* for the people who suffer them. As for those who see others in painful situations, *they too* may very well think of the meaning which these others could easily attach to their present situation, and then wish to improve it with *that* special aspect in mind. Things are not always that clear, of course; and yet, when facing the condition of the unemployed, the poor, or the underpriviledged, many people would often want to say: "Something *must* be done! Those people just don't *deserve* such a life! Above all, they don't deserve having to interpret their situation as a proof that they aren't at all *qualified* to live as happy as the others, as happy as *ourselves*!..."

One would now have to discover what it is, more exactly, that these unemployed, or poor, or underpriviledged people desire so much, that they often couldn't help *fearing* that their own condition might very well mean what they suspected all the time, and could therefore *appreciate* — so very much — the fact that others finally acknowledged them as "deserving" to live a happy life. It is often easy to see that the underpriviledged people value all the more the help of the others, when they can see in it a *new* sign, one which tended to evict another one and corresponded, this time, to a desire of theirs which the previous sign only exasperated, and even threatened to extinguish once and for all. That a few underpriviledged persons became able to live a much happier life, but only because other people had simply pulled them out of their difficult condition, *that* fact isn't particularly encouraging or gratifying for them. (Such a "deed" could even be felt as something a bit humiliating for them, and confirm the suspicion they already had of not being *themselves* capable, in fact, of living a happy life...) But that the others had acted so as to put an end to a situation which these other people *themselves* considered as definitely *abnormal* (and had therefore acted out of consideration for persons who they thought didn't deserve such a painful condition), now *that* fact is no doubt something the underpriviledged people can appreciate, and something their persons *themselves* could especially appreciate. For that is precisely *the* improvement of the situation they were really hoping for all along, that is, the possibility of having their "personally" happy life emerge, and start flowing again, and above all, the possiblity for their own *persons* simply to "breathe".

Having already experienced anxieties of that kind, most people could easily suspect, in fact, that the improvement which the underpriviledged persons particularly hope for — especially the destitute and the castoff — is one which concerns their "person" itself, that is, that component of their entire being which *primarily* constitutes them, and without which they, themselves, couldn't be *what* they are, or, more precisely, *who* they are. During the periods in which the underpriviledged believe that their condition could be *permanent,* it becomes clear — at least for the people who actually meet them often enough — that it is their own persons *as such* who falter, who are lacking in vitality, and who would no doubt need an *appropriate* nourishment. But this "nourishment" could only be, in fact, a certain *sign*, one which would be convincing enough to actually rid these persons of the doubts they have about their own selves, and therefore a sign which would have to come from other persons, that is, from beings who were able to make them *experience* their own capacity to live as happy *persons*.

It is only through a particular kind of sign, indeed, that others could make these persons realize that they, themselves, are *recognized* as deserving a happy life, and could thus convince them of already having, within themselves, "all that it takes" to *deserve* the respect and consideration of the others, and to live as happy *persons*. When people happen to perceive such a sign, then their doubts and apprehensions are apt to vanish, since they are again reassured about the object of their most fundamental and urgent desire. They already feel themselves living "out of the very depth" (as they might say) of their own persons, quite happy because of that, and even capable of being patient in situations which can still be difficult, of course, yet not paralyzing any more, nor as unbearably painful.

To acknowledge the fact that the underpriviledged people "don't deserve" their painful and distressing condition is to recognize, at the same time — but not always with the utmost awareness —, that it is their own *persons* who don't deserve that "abnormal" condition, and who especially don't deserve to bear it any longer. If it so happened that others felt themselves *obliged* to do something about it, that would be because these others had felt somehow *responsible,* at that moment, for what it might perhaps *mean*, for those underpriviledged people, that other people actually *wanted* to improve their condition, *or* that no one even wanted to *try* to do so... And perhaps responsible, at the same time, for the fact that these people became able to emerge and to live as *persons*, or for the fact that, on the contrary, their persons might have to keep on declining, for want of appropriate "nourishment". But should one think that the underprivileged and the destitute are the only human beings who would need such a nourishment for their *persons*?

Every time people want to improve the social condition, it would seem that they only think of the needy, the underpriviledged, or the poor. Isn't it only for the sake of these unfortunate people, in fact, that an improvement must be introduced? Who else would really *need* a change? They also think of the more prosperous citizens of course, and of all those who manage quite well, but only as of those who would be able to improve the condition of the others, and should therefore have the job of doing so. But many of these people don't seem to realize what they actually *require* of the richer citizens, as if it went without saying that such a task would never involve anything painful, nor any risk at all regarding the happy future of the richer citizens themselves. According to them, everything is all very simple, since "noblesse oblige" (isn't that right?), and since fulfilling that task already contains its reward anyway. And that's it, period!

Now supposing that conception were right, would it concern the improvement of the conditions of *society* itself, or that of *some* of its members only, that is, of the underpriviledged citizens? Can one actually think that the rich also improve *their own* condition, when they improve that of the poor? If not, then how could one reconcile such a way of seeing things, with the widespread idea — an idea not so very consistent itself — that human beings live in a society for the benefit of *all* the citizens? What *benefit*, indeed, could the well-off and the more resourceful citizens actually *acquire* from having to live in a society where the poor and the underpriviledged were so numerous?

If one remained convinced that the rich themselves would benefit by improving the condition of the poor, is it because the latter wouldn't be tempted any more to steal from them, to harass or annoy them in all sorts of ways, nor to think of starting some kind of revolution which could perhaps dispossess them for good? Or would the reason be that once the rich had actually improved the condition of *all* the poor and the destitute, the latter could finally live a decent life without having to disturb anyone, and without anyone having to accomplish, any more, such a painful and irksome task in favor of a bunch of totally "incompetent" people? Of course, in a sense, the rich would also be among the beneficiaries of the improvement in question. But could such an improvement be accomplished *in time,* that is, before *they* died? (Could they really believe that?) If not, could they be sufficiently motivated by the thought that their own children, at least, would benefit from that improvement? In any case, could one truly say, about the human beings living in a group in which (at last?) none of them needed the others, that they would be living in a "society", and not just "in contact" with each other? Incidentally, what does that actually *mean*, to live "in a society"? And what would be the particular benefit that *each* of the members could acquire, by living in a "society"?

To start with, one could note that the presence of the underpriviledged and the poor, within a society, can certainly be a very good occasion for the others to be reminded of the most characteristic need of their *persons* (in fact, of *all* persons). It is indeed quite natural that the painful condition of the poorest, and their observable distress, should call to mind, in a specially dramatic way, their need for a particularly indispensable "sustenance", that is, for the actual recognition, by the others, of the fact that they were truly qualified to live as happy *persons*. But if the others can sometimes sense *that* need of the poor, it is no doubt because they are already familiar with it. Some may remember quite clearly having experienced it themselves, may even feel it is still there (although not too urgent for the moment), and may suspect that they, too, could once again start feeling its painful insistance (perhaps this time forever?). And if, having begun to help some of these unfortunate people, they suddenly notice that they, themselves, experience a particularly peaceful and gratifying well-being, that is presumably because their own persons have emerged (and continue to live) as *persons*; and that, in turn, is no doubt because they had freely chosen to help those unfortunate people "out of a true consideration" for *their* persons.

If it is true that people cannot live a "fundamentally" happy life — that is, one which would be happy in spite of all sorts of inevitable pains — without their own persons, as such, being "active"; and if it is also a fact that the only appropriate and indispensable "nourishment" for the life of their person is a true consideration coming from the others (or from their own selves, for others), it then becomes obvious that everyone actually needs *the others* in order to live as a person, and as a happy one. It thus seems that for *all* human beings there should always be other people around, from which they could obtain the right "nourishment" for their own persons — especially when they most needed it! —, or to which they could offer the same kind of sustenance (while being morally obliged, sometimes, to do so).

It is in that sense — or because of that particular need of the person itself —, that everyone would have to live in a "society". One can see quite clearly what the benefit would then be, for each and *every one* of the persons, provided only that "living in a society" consisted in people not just living together, but living together *as persons*, and therefore out of a true *consideration* for each other. In a real "society", everyone's consideration should actually be directed towards *all* its members, and not just towards some of them, however numerous...

Indeed, a true consideration for *persons* could never be aimed at some of them, with the explicit exception of others. When persons are living out of (or with) consideration for a particular individual, then, of course, they often think of that individual only, while doing what they do, saying what they say, and so on. But if one of the reasons why they *could* freely choose to make themselves *have* a personal consideration for that individual, is that they had somehow realized that he, or she, was a *person* (or *could* be a person), then their personal attitude towards that individual is essentially *the same* as the one they would have, if they were making themselves have a true consideration for this or that *other* person, or for *any* other persons, whether they actually knew them or not.

In other words, one could also note that no one could, *at the same time*, be acting and living out of a truly personal consideration for certain members of society, and *refuse* to have the same kind of attitude towards other members. (Such a denial — or mere personal *indifference* towards these others — would indeed put an end to any already existing consideration for certain people, while putting a stop, at the same time, to the personal *life* of the one who refused.) The life of anyone's person *itself* would thus be an eminently *social* one, no one having the capacity to *exclude* any other person from the consideration (for others) which maintains his or her *own* person, as such, alive. And so that same life (of anyone's person) is necessarily incompatible with any form of real individualism, with any contempt towards others, with any denial of personal responsibility — and even with any personal indifference — regarding persons or groups of persons.

How would it then be possible to *improve* our life within a "society"? If such a life is in fact that of people living together as *persons*, there are no doubt quite a few ways of improving the actual conditions of such a life. But each of them would finally consist in maintaining, or restoring, all that would appear more apt to bring about the real possibility, for everyone, to live as persons, that is, as beings who deserve the personal consideraton of *all* the others, and who should be responsible for the same consideration towards *all* the others. More apt, in other words, to promote the concrete expression of a mutual consideration between all persons, or the most universal circulation of this indispensable "nourishment" of the persons themselves.

That type of improvement — as opposed to the improvement of the simple well-being of everyone — is always *possible*. It is actually pointed out to each person, when he or she feels a moral obligation, or responsibility, involving his or her *present* consideration towards others. But the most urgent task — sometimes a very difficult one — is no doubt that of an active and convincing expression, by means of *observable* facts, of each and everyone's consideration for all the others. Even if we often insist on the fact that "authentic" attitudes are demonstrated not by mere words, but by "tangible" acts and productions, it still remains that, in very many cases, *language* is an indispensable complement, or even the only means one could use. But an obsessive craving for the constant *efficiency* of our efforts and activities often conceals that fact, and even the very presence of the persons themselves... Still, there are moments when only *words* can actually manifest one's true consideration for the people who are expecting it, and can be "efficient" in having them really *sense* this consideration, for them, which "efficiently" allows them to emerge and to "breathe", not only as persons, but also as happy persons.

The particular improvement of the social situation by means of "actively expressed consideration" is not only a possible improvement. It *already* takes place. It does so each time the true consideration of certain people towards others is actually *perceived* by the latter, since their own *persons* then "emerge", and society thus acquires a new source of possible consideration (and of "personal" life) for *all* its members. Some of these sources — and even each one of them, at certain times or for certain periods — will again be deprived of their "personal" life, sometimes by accident, sometimes by their own choice (having freely chosen to *withhold* their personal consideration for others). But during those periods, the consideration of the others, towards *them*, might enable them to emerge and to live again as persons, and as persons happy to become sources, once more, of consideration (and personal life) for others.

At any rate, it does seem, quite often, that something very similar to this particular kind of improvement of "life in society", is precisely what most citizens happen to long for (more or less consciously), whether they were poor *or* rich, "communitarians" *or* individualists.

The promotion of mutual aid

The question which guided the present research and study is clear enough: "What could citizens expect, from their government, regarding life within their own society?". It is obvious that such a question cannot interest those who have come to expect nothing else, from their political rulers, than lies, injustice, and a constant misuse of power. On the other hand, one can well imagine how it could still interest the poor, the destitute, and the cast-off who have refused to abandon all hope. At any rate, it certainly preoccupies many citizens who suspect — no doubt correctly — that there will always *exist* a political power, yet who persist in believing that it should be *possible* for a government, in spite of all the difficulties, to fulfill a valuable social function.

That belief doesn't seem realistic at all. How, indeed, *could* one imagine a government"s policies — even among the best — as producing anything else but effects which would be *sometimes* beneficial (but for a few groups of citizens only), yet *more often* hurtful for a great number of citizens, including the less fortunate ones? Even when only the "perverse" effects of government policies are considered, any government may no doubt be compared to all those other "forces of nature" which, like the sun and heavy rains, or the animal world, often "behave" in ways that are beneficial for human beings, but also — and always too often! — in ways that produce disastrous effects (heatwaves, floods, damages caused by insects or rats, and so on).Because of the perverse effects of government policies, but also because of the deviations which occult pressure groups impose on these policies, it appears that no citizen could expect anything more, from them, than a succession of periods some of which would be fairly happy ones, but others mostly painful, or very difficult. In other words, no citizen is ever in a position to expect, from any government, what he or she often does in fact expect, that is, a certain *security* concerning his or her own well-being, and much less that of all the citizens.

Some would no doubt want to be more realistic and so expect nothing more, from their government, than a partial and inevitably insufficient security, yet one whose extension and efficiency would constantly increase. (They consider this as a "mere" improvement, but an improvement anyway.) Isn't it true, after all, that the political rulers — as all human beings — are forces of nature capable of directing and controlling other such forces, and above all of anticipating and preventing the perverse effects of their own activities, at least up to a certain point? It still remains a fact, however, that with regard to whatever each and every one of the citizens is *most* intent on doing or obtaining, only the thoughtless or the particularly naive could be content with a type of security which would be only "partially" efficient. (Besides, would an intermittent or partial security actually deserve to be considered as a true *security*, especially when what is at stake is the *enduring* well-being of each citizen, and their protection against any kind of serious damages?)

One should also note that a government would be all the more *incapable* of meeting the expectation of a greater security concerning various types of well-being, as this expectation is often (as we have seen) an expression of the need for a particular kind of "nourishment", that which would enable the persons themselves to live a happy life, or to prosper as *persons*. (Many people find it rather surprising that even the wealthier citizens often feel very insecure, and apparently unable to see in the abundance of their personal possessions, or in the well-being they actually enjoy, that which would allow them to consider themselves as happy *and* secure persons. This particular feeling of insecurity is no doubt what nevertheless keeps them from wanting to disengage themselves from their possessions, or from leaving aside part of their own well-being, in favor of the less fortunate citizens.) If it really *is* this "personal" and often misapprehended insecurity which actually urges many citizens to expect, from their governments, a greater security with regard to their daily well-being, then no government, of course, could ever fulfill this expectation, even by means of its most efficient policies. But does that mean that no government could ever do anything at all to *participate*, at least, in the improvement of the *social* life (and therefore the "personal" life) of all the citizens?

Among the liberal intellectuals, many recognize this incapacity, for any government, to promote the "flourishing" of the persons themselves. (And just too bad — or so it would seem — if that particular flourishing happened to be precisely the object of the principal preoccupation of most citizens...) These intellectuals have therefore preferred to fall back upon the promotion of the "minimal state" — the "night-watchman state" —, whose function would only consist in protecting individuals against acts of injustice committed by the others. What more could the state do, indeed, given the fact that the *variety* of things which the citizens would apparently need for the vitality of their own persons is so great, and so often divergent and even clashing, that no one could ever accept that *certain* citizens decided for the others — and much less for all — about the concrete (and limited) ways the fulfillment of this need should be pursued?

As for the social-minded intellectuals, they too have finally admitted, but for other reasons and with a certain regret, that a government is quite unable to promote the flourishing of each individual, mostly for lack of sufficient goods and resources for all (or for lack of a boundless increase in production), and because of a certain number of "perverse" effects, among which the seemingly unavoidable inefficiency of an indispensable bureaucracy. And so it appears that the political thinkers — the socialists just as well as the liberals — have been condemned to completely dissociate from each other the private and the public domains, and to concentrate all government efficiency on the proper functioning of the *public* sector only, and no matter what might happen, as a result, to the vitality of the persons themselves. Of course, the difficulty always remains of finding the *efficient* means — or at least the most appropriate ones — to articulate the concrete relations between the government or the political authorities, on the one hand, and society *itself*, on the other hand, that is, the totality of *all* the persons. And that difficulty is even more insurmountable when there is no social *consensus* — as is the case right now — concerning the role of the government, justice (social or individual), values, and the happy life.

Now this difficulty would certainly not be the same any more, and could be tackled with much more hope, if the governments of our democratic societies would finally consider themselves — and if the citizens also considered *them* — as groups of persons who were *themselves* a part of these societies, and whose essential aim were to promote a *mutual* aid. A government, then, wouldn't be "above" the citizens, or "above" society itself any more, nor endowed with a very special power and authority, somehow "superhuman" and boundless. (Many citizens believe nothing of the sort about their political rulers, yet don't seem to realize how often they think and behave as if they did...) The members of such a government would actually live as other citizens do, or as citizens who are perhaps stronger and more able (in some respects) than many others, and therefore capable, for example, of offering *more* help to those who are in trouble.

The typical activities of that government would not consist in helping each of the underpriviledged citizens to take care of himself or herself (by means of a social welfare check?), but rather in helping all of them to *help each other*, within their own local and "natural" groups. That concrete aid could consist in supplying with the necessary means those of the citizens who, whether they were well-off or not, would like to help the needy to help themselves *mutually*. (Such a policy already exists in many places, but the idea is still considered as a side issue, and often as a temporary substitute.) One can certainly imagine that once taken seriously and closely attended to, that type of government aid would not necessarily provoke the angry disapproval of the other citizens. On the contrary, one can anticipate that these other citizens would entertain the hope that, together, the needy would become more imaginative, more resourceful, and actually succeed in pulling themselves out of their unhappy situation — thus alleviating their own tax burden, and perhaps also their social conscience... Furthermore, a government could reinforce that hope by publicizing some of the more striking success stories and obtain, for that kind of government aid, a much greater consensus among the more prosperous taxpayers.

However, one could ask whether that type of government policy would promote a mutual aid which would be a truly *social* one, that is, a mutual aid between *all* the members of society. Wouldn't the government stand, here again, above society itself, or outside of it? Could we say, about the underpriviledged citizens who lived under such a social structure, that *they too* were actually helping the members of their government? Would they be helping the taxpayers, or at least the persons with whom they were in contact, and who were helping them to help each other? As for these persons, what are *they* doing, when trying to promote mutual aid among the underprivileged and the poor? Only "breakdown" service? Only helping them to help each other — provisionally of course — to stand on their own feet, and finally become able to "function", each by himself or herself *alone*, like all the other citizens? Is the aim of politics, of life within society, of the aid brought by certain citizens to others, always that all the citizens should succeed, one of these days, in living in a truly *autonomous* way, that is, quite *independently* of the others, so that no important mutual aid (concerning anything whatever) would ever be required any more?

At any rate, it isn't at all sure that the word "freedom", when used in the context of the most absorbing preoccupation of the citizens, would mean "autonomy", or the fact of being independent of all the others in *every* respect. On the contrary, it would seem — as we have already noticed — that what both the poor *and* the rich people need above all, when they feel particularly distressed or miserable (and not only the victims of painful situations) is not so much a greater amount of autonomy or independence — that is, more "negative" liberty —, but preferably a really "positive" liberty, that which would be required for their own persons to live precisely as *persons*. For that is indeed the type of liberty which would allow them to live what they then need to live: exchanges of mutual "consideration", or concern, aptly manifested by observable acts and behavior.

We have already perceived the reason why exchanges of that kind, among citizens, cannot possibly exclude *any* member[11] of the particular community they happen to produce, to maintain, and often to regenerate (especially within those of its members who feel a more urgent need for that personal "nourishment"). This society of persons *living* as persons[12] — or society at its distinctive best — cannot therefore avoid being a society of *mutual aid*. Of mutual aid between *all* the citizens, each one of them feeling the need sometimes to be the object of the consideration or respect of the others (which would allow them to arise as persons), or sometimes to direct towards others a consideration whose mere *production*, expressed within observable acts and behavior, would allow them to sustain or revive the *life* (and happiness) of their own persons.

One can understand, then, how the political rulers — as well as all the men and women who help other citizens engage in mutual and considerate aid — can remain (or become) parts of a society of mutual aid between *all* the citizens. Those who receive the concrete and considerate help happen to aid the ones who help them, if only by offering them the *particularly* concrete possibility of acting (and

---

[11] Even if their life or *behavior* hardly seems to be that of actual persons, yet killers, brutes, fetuses, vicious teenagers, heartless exploiters of all kinds, and so on, are *also* persons, and would therefore have a right to the consideration of all the others. Or there is the risk, at least, that they *were* persons. (In that case, what would it *mean* to choose to behave, towards these beings, as if they were not persons at all?...)

[12] This could perhaps be compared to the *kingdom of ends*, that is, the community of *persons* which Kant had conceived in a purely formal way, and which, because of that, cannot be recognized as corresponding to the most characteristic preoccupation of the *persons* themselves.

living) out of consideration for other persons. But once effectively helped, the receivers will no doubt happen to feel, at times, the need to help others more actively. On the other hand, one can anticipate that the citizens who help others more often — because of their situation or their particular capacities — will certainly experience the need, sooner or later, to be themselves the object of the consideration of the others. (Although it has been said that "there is *more* joy in giving than in receiving", it still remains a fact that the person of each citizen often needs to *receive* its appropriate nourishment. The saying can't mean there should be *no* great joy in receiving such a nourishment...)

There is no doubt there will always be people who are poor, who struggle or simply despair in the midst of very difficult situations. As for those who could be suspected of being outright lazy, or plain hypocrites, no one can be sure they have *not* been forced to that kind of life by a lack of sufficient "sustenance" for their own persons. But because of their stark visibility, the poor, the helpless, and the saddening destitute — of whichever kind — often force the rich to become more aware of *their own* lack of "personal" nourishment, more aware of the present (or near) "poverty" of their own persons. Actually this poverty, this precariousness of the life of one's person itself seems to attain *all* the citizens, more or less frequently, and at least to some degree. The blatantly underpriviledged, however, are often a more effective reminder of the *fundamental insecurity* of all human beings, as regards their actual capacity to live as *persons*. Far from being only a burden for society, the poor and the destitute — especially those who ask for help — do their fellow citizens a good turn in allowing them to discover and rediscover, *more surely,* the most effective way of improving the social situation for *all* the citizens, and more particularly, of course, for the ones who actually help them. As already noted, a social improvement is a real one, if it consists in the promotion of a *general* mutual aid, that is, a more extensive circulation, within society, of a true "consideration" for the persons themselves. And there is no doubt that this type of improvement is always *practicable*, if only by a few members of society at a time.

* * *

Our study of a certain number of common human experiences has brought out the following points and relations:

1) No individual could live as a *person* — or as someone living the life of his or her own *free* choice — without having a minimum of "consideration", or respect, for other persons.

   That means that no one could live *as a person* while having freely chosen to be "contemptuous" towards others. Furthermore, when someone acts out of contempt, he or she is then (and only then) doing something *unjust*.

   Therefore, the "object" to which, above all, every individual has a *right* with regard to all the others, is that they had a minimum of consideration, or respect, towards his or her own person itself. Individuals also have the right to *anything* which the others couldn't possibly deny them (at the moment) without freely choosing to have contempt for their persons.

2) Individuals are living a "fundamentally" happy life, when they are in the way of obtaining or doing what they are *most intent* on obtaining or doing. For in such cases, their happiness is not at all destroyed by the various kinds of harms and annoyances they still have to suffer.

   Whenever individuals happen to feel particularly miserable despite the fact that everything seems to be going quite well, that is often because their persons *themselves* are incapable of living what *they* would be most intent on living. Their own persons, as such, would be in need of an appropriate "nourishment". It does seem, however, that this nourishment could only be the particular experience which usually occurs when the person *itself* is the object of the consideration or respect of other persons, or is making itself have, or maintain, a true consideration for other persons.

   Individuals can therefore live as persons when what they do, they do out of (or with) consideration for other persons. They would then be living an at least "fundamentally" happy life, since they would be living, in the concrete everyday world, the life which *they* were freely (and personally) intent on living.

3) Since it is only for persons *as such*, that human beings could make themselves have a freely chosen consideration or respect, it would be totally *impossible*, for them, to be living or acting out of a true consideration for certain persons (or groups), while having a freely chosen *contempt* towards other members of their society (who are *also* persons). These two attitudes, or dispositions, towards persons, just cannot be held at the same time.

To live with (or out of) a true consideration or respect for any member of society, is thus to live for *all* the members of society, or for society *as a whole*. Once a citizen has freely chosen to be considerate and respectful towards all other persons, then he or she can indeed play an important part in the emergence, the sustenance, or the renewal of the "personal" life of all the citizens, and in the vitalization, therefore, of the mutual concern which constitutes the very life of a genuine *society*. But that distinctive participation would naturally consist in promoting a concrete mutual *aid*, the most convincing manifestation of the *existence* of a true consideration between all the citizens.

Promoting this mutual aid — or maintaining this general readiness to supply concrete aid — would then consist, for each individual, in sustaining the life of his or her *own* free person, and in living fundamentally happy, since "personally" happy. But that, of course, would be living a life quite different from the kind offered by strict individualism, a conception which seems implicitly bent on promoting the "anemia" — or the actual "death"? — of each basically "independent" person.

Taken into account, the foregoing clarifications, arguments, and interpretations (all "non normative"), may enable one to propose a *realistic* answer to the initial question: "What could the citizens expect, from their governments, as policies which were clearly for the benefit of *all* the members of their society?". Whatever it may be, that answer is certainly not the *security* of the citizens against all that could threaten their life, their peacefulness, their possessions, or their capacity to accomplish — without harming others! — the projects they would be most intent on realizing. For no government could even really *improve* the social situation with respect to any of these matters, except perhaps for a certain number of citizens, and for a certain time.

Moreover, there is something ridiculous about the statement: "One must leave nothing to *chance*. Or as little as possible!". We have already noted, indeed, that for any particular action or omission — including those of the best possible governments —, it could only be the result of *chance*, in the end, if the totality of their consequences (especially the more distant ones) turned out to be happy *or* unhappy ones. If, however, a great number of citizens still insisted on judging useful (or quite reasonable) that their government tried to *improve* things, then it is obvious that such an improvement couldn't concern the impossible *security* of their concrete daily lives.

As the present study has shown, the only thing that the members of a government could do to improve the *social* condition, is to try to fulfill the most fundamental desire of the citizens[13] by doing all the things they do — they can't *avoid* doing all sorts of things! — *mostly* out of (or with) a truly personal consideration for *all* the citizens. (And that motive, that consideration, would have to be as visible or convincing as possible for every citizen!) Now if that were in fact the principal aim of the political rulers, then they would be *publicly* promoting a mutual consideration — and an *effective* mutual aid — among all the citizens, while living, at the same time, a "personally" happy life. In other words, they would be promoting the vitality of the *social bond* itself, the vitality of a true *society*. (Or promoting the so-called "common good", which could finally be seen as both "good" *and* "common"...)[14]

That, then, is what a "well-disposed" government could do; and what it would always be *capable* of doing. It is also, of course, what the other citizens could realistically expect from their government. In fact, it is even what many

---

13 This could perhaps be compared to the *kingdom of ends*, that is, the community of *persons* which Kant had conceived in a purely formal way, and which, because of that, cannot be recognized as corresponding to the most characteristic preoccupation of the *persons* themselves.

14 Many contemporary writers in philosophical or theoretical politics have offered stimulating ideas on the politics and ethics of life *in society*, whether they were more liberal-minded (R.Dworkin, R.Nozick), consensus-minded (J.Rawls), solidarity or community-minded (M.Walzer, A.MacIntyre, R.Rorty). But probably because of a seemingly unshakeable visceral attitude concerning so-called *substantive* and *obscure* (or metaphysical?) subjects, they still cannot allow themselves to study the implicitly experienced *needs* and *rights* of the persons as such, thus depriving themselves of a source of understanding and explanation, and of the possibility of finding more convincing *practical* criteria for the solution of political and ethical problems.

citizens already do expect from their political rulers, although more or less consciously, and without a very firm confidence...

One might be under the impression that the *political* role of the government has just been reduced to almost nothing. Or to something rather "ethereal", something "nice and sweet", or much too sentimental (this "consideration" for persons!). One might also object to a conception of "life in society" which seemed to imagine the citizens as constantly exchanging tokens of "gentle" consideration, or perhaps as dancing in a ring, *all* of them smiling and holding each other's hand: beggars and managing directors, cellists and stocky mobsters, olympic champions and tottering invalids. But should one really try to answer such superficial objections? (Are they true objections, or expressions of moody unfairness?) Has one never sensed that it is precisely a need for this so-called "ethereal" or "sugar-coated" consideration, which has nevertheless *killed*, or *paralyzed* the "personal" life of many people, and is still doing so every day? Has no one ever had the occasion to notice, as yet, that the same need, once exasperated, is also what often drives people to a behavior which could hardly be considered "ethereal" — such as murder, rape, or the cruel exploitation of the helpless? Besides, why should one think — as many people apparently do! — that an individual who had a sincere consideration for another couldn't *possibly* give him something as unethereal as a good swift kick in the rear end?...[15]

Having finally realized the importance of the function the political rulers could actually perform in the midst of their fellow citizens — the promotion of a mutual and "considerate" *aid* among all the members of society —, one shouldn't underestimate, on the other hand, the *symbolic* function they could also perform. (Yet another "vaporous" thing?) Since a great number of citizens are strongly impressed by the apparently *supreme* power of their government, they cannot help perceiving it as a group of individuals particularly capable of steering the course of their common destiny for the better, but also for *the worse*. And so would it seem that the political rulers are naturally called upon to make sure they became a more

[15] Perhaps the footwork appeared to the first individual as the only way, in the circumstances, to prevent a couple of small children from getting seriously hurt. (He probably intended to explain that to his victim, afterwards, adding that he had no lack of respect, no contempt at all towards him, and was really sorry...)

reassuring symbol, mostly by *publicly* (and frequently) proclaiming the respect to which *every* citizen had a right — they would thus be simply reaffirming the foremost intent of their country's Constitution —, but perhaps even more by publicly expressing (and reviving?) the *sincerity* of their own consideration for each and every citizen. At any rate, that would certainly be one way they could effectively compensate, by words or meaningful gestures, for the inevitable inefficiency of their current policies. (One could hardly say that the sincerity of our political rulers is always obvious or very convincing, even during preelection years...)

The only thing which the citizens could expect from their government is then the one — the *only* one — their political rulers would have the *capacity* of supplying: policies meant to encourage mutual aid between all the citizens, that is, the improvement of life in a true *society*. (Such policies would of course have to express, as convincingly as possible, a true consideration of the political rulers for each and every one of their *fellow* citizens.) It seems that many citizens already do expect (more or less consciously) the coming of a society of mutually "considerate" aid, and that the "social democratic", the "communitarian", the "communicational", and the "solidarity-minded" theorists have noticed that fact, as well as the extraordinary importance of that particular kind of aid, with regard to the life of the persons (as such), and with regard to the life of our society itself. (The citizens who rather fear — for themselves! — the advent of a society of *mutual* aid, wouldn't dare say so, and will probably never take the risk of publicly setting themselves against it...)

In any case, it would certainly be of great service to everyone, if the necessary link were recognized between justice, non-contempt (or consideration), and mutual aid, as well as the particular relation between life in society, free choices, and the "fundamentaly" happy life of each person. But even though the government were to fulfill its "actively symbolic" role, and the citizens were mutually helpful (without too many faults or offenses), the fact would still remain that an enigmatic *haphazardness* would continue to determine the course of our personal and social history... Our lives, therefore, will always remain an *adventure*, the only saving reaction to it being, at times, a most tenacious *hope*. One can see, then, that the best type of mutual and *social* aid would consist in *no one* ever killing, ever even undermining, in the least, that often fragile hope of the persons themselves. But rather, on the contrary, in having it become more encouragingly intense by fulfilling, whenever possible — each citizen for the benefit of any of the others —, the promise which that hope already seems to contain.

INDEX

About the author

Gilles Lane is professor of philosophy at the University of Montreal. He has published books, in French, on sense perception, objectivity, scientific knowledge, the significance of philosophy, and, more recently, on the fundamental problems of ethics, life in society, and politics.

In 1970, he published *Quand dire, c'est faire* (Paris, Seuil), a French translation of J.L. Austin's *How To Do Things With Words*, to which he added an Introduction and a Commentary. A pocket edition came out in 1991.